How To Use This Study Guide

This ten-lesson study guide corresponds to *"How To Stay in a Place of Faith" With Rick Renner* (Renner TV). Each lesson in this study guide covers a topic that is addressed during the program series, with questions and references supplied to draw you deeper into your own private study of the Scriptures on this subject.

To derive the most benefit from this study guide, consider the following:

First, watch or listen to the program prior to working through the corresponding lesson in this guide. (Programs can also be viewed at **renner.org** by clicking on the Media/Archives links or on our Renner Ministries YouTube channel.)

Second, take the time to look up the scriptures included in each lesson. Prayerfully consider their application to your own life.

Third, use a journal or notebook to make note of your answers to each lesson's Study Questions and Practical Application challenges.

Fourth, invest specific time in prayer and in the Word of God to consult with the Holy Spirit. Write down the scriptures or insights He reveals to you.

Finally, take action! Whatever the Lord tells you to do according to His Word, do it.

For added insights on this subject, it is recommended that you obtain Rick Renner's book *Dream Thieves: Overcoming Obstacles To Fulfill Your Dreams*. You may also select from Rick's other available resources by placing your order at **renner.org** or by calling 1-800-742-5593.

TOPIC

Why Hold On to God's Promise?

SCRIPTURES

1. **Hebrews 10:23** — Let us hold fast the profession of our faith without wavering; (for he is faithful that promised).

2. **Romans 1:18** — For the wrath of God is revealed from heaven against all ungodliness and unrighteousness of men, who hold the truth in unrighteousness.

3. **2 Thessalonians 2:6** — And now ye know what withholdeth that he might be revealed in his time.

4. **1 John 1:9** — If we confess our sins, he is faithful and just to forgive us our sins, and to cleanse us from all unrighteousness.

5. **1 Peter 2:24** — ...By whose stripes ye were healed.

GREEK WORDS

1. "hold fast" — **κατέχω** (*katecho*): a compound of the words **κατά** (*kata*) and ἔχω (*echo*); the word **κατά** (*kata*) means down, and ἔχω (*echo*) means to have, to hold fast, or to possess; it pictures someone who has something in his possession and is holding it down or suppressing it; as a compound, the new word **κατέχω** (*katecho*) means to restrain, to hold back, or to suppress

2. "hold" — **κατέχω** (*katecho*): a compound of the words **κατά** (*kata*) and ἔχω (*echo*); the word **κατά** (*kata*) means down, and ἔχω (*echo*) means to have, to hold fast, or to possess; it pictures someone who has something in his possession and is holding it down or suppressing it; as a compound, the new word **κατέχω** (*katecho*) means to restrain, to hold back, or to suppress

3. "withholdeth" — **κατέχω** (*katecho*): a compound of the words **κατά** (*kata*) and ἔχω (*echo*); the word **κατά** (*kata*) means down, and ἔχω (*echo*) means to have, to hold fast, or to possess; it pictures someone who has something in his possession and is holding it down or suppressing it; as a compound, the new word **κατέχω** (*katecho*) means to restrain, to hold back, or to suppress

4. "profession" — ὁμολογίαν (*homologian*): a compound word derived from the word ὁμολογέω (*homologeo*), which is made up of the words ὁμός (*homos*), which means one of the very same kind, and λογέω (*logeo*), meaning I say; when compounded, ὁμολογίαν (*homologian*) means to say the same thing; to agree

5. "faith" — ἐλπίδος (*elpidos*): derived from the word ἐλπίς (*elpis*), which is the word for hope or expectation; a full expectation that what God has promised will come to pass

6. "without wavering" — ἀκλινῆς (*aklines*): derived from the Greek prefix α (*a*), meaning not or without and has a cancelling effect, and κλίνω (*klino*), which means to recline or to go to bed; it describes one who yields, one who surrenders, one who gives up ground or surrenders territory; when α (*a*) is added to the beginning of κλίνω (*klino*), the new word, ἀκλινής (*aklines*), means do not yield, do not surrender, do not go to bed, do not recline, do not surrender territory

SYNOPSIS

The ten lessons in this study titled, *How To Stay in a Place of Faith* will focus on the following topics:

- Why Hold On to God's Promise?
- What's Trying To Steal Your Dream?
- Why Do We Need Each Other?
- Are You Close to Your Harvest?
- Is the Enemy Fighting Your Light?
- Are You Standing Your Ground?
- Will You Shine Under Scrutiny?
- Are You Bold Enough To Wait?
- Is Your Faith Growing or Rotting?
- Will Your Faith Change the Future?

The emphasis of this lesson:

To see God's promises become a reality in our lives, we must learn to hold fast to them. This means holding them down, suppressing them, and putting all our spiritual weight on top of them so that the enemy,

circumstances, or life itself can't take them from us. Holding fast to our confession of faith brings us into divine alignment with God.

What Does It Mean To 'Hold Fast'?

The book of Hebrews is addressed to a group of Jews who had been attacked in their faith and were really struggling. They were suffering so severely that they were questioning their faith in Christ and were tempted to let go of it. To encourage his readers, the writer said:

> **Let us hold fast the profession of our faith without wavering; (for he is faithful that promised).**
> — **Hebrews 10:23**

There are several important words to understand in this verse, including the words "hold fast," "profession," "faith," and "wavering." As we unpack the meaning of these words, you'll see God's message for everyone who is holding on to His promises in faith.

First, the writer of Hebrews began by saying, "Let us hold fast the profession of our faith…" (Hebrews 10:23). In Greek, the words "hold fast" are a form of the word *katecho*, which is a compound of the words *kata* and *echo*. The word *kata* describes *something coming down, conquering,* or *dominating* while *echo* means *to have, to hold,* or *to possess.* When these two words are compounded to form *katecho*, it pictures *someone who has something in his or her possession, and he or she is holding it down or suppressing it.*

Two Examples of *Katecho* in Scripture

The New Testament has several examples of the use of this word *katecho*. The two verses we are going to examine are Romans 1:18 and Second Thessalonians 2:6.

In **Romans 1:18**, Paul wrote, "For the wrath of God is revealed from heaven against all ungodliness and unrighteousness of men, who *hold* the truth in unrighteousness." In this verse, the word "hold" is the Greek word *katecho*, which again means *to hold down* or *to suppress.* In this case, Paul was talking about ungodly men who have the truth, but because they don't like it, they're trying to hold it down, suppress it, and put a lid on it lest it get out and affect people.

Interestingly, that is exactly what we see happening very often in our world today, especially in the media and the press. When they don't like the truth, they "sit on a story" by hiding it, suppressing it, holding it down, and restraining it. That's what this word "hold" means.

A second example is found in **Second Thessalonians 2:6**, which says, "And now ye know what *withholdeth* that he might be revealed in his time." In this verse and in verse 7, the apostle Paul was describing the "great restrainer" that is at work in the earth at the end of the age, and he said the restrainer "withholdeth" something. That word "withholdeth" is again the Greek word *katecho*, which could be translated *to restrain*, *to hold back*, or *to suppress*.

Here, *katecho* pictures one who is putting all his might and weight onto something so he can hold it down and stop it from moving or being released. This is a picture of the Church in the last of the last days. We are the great *restrainer*, and part of our role in this world is to restrain evil. We are called to suppress it, hold it down, and put a lid on it so it doesn't get away and begin to affect the entire human race. All this meaning is in the word *katecho*.

Be Determined To Never Let Go
of God's Promises

Returning to our anchor verse in Hebrews 10:23, it says, "Let us hold fast the profession of our faith…." A good translation of this verse would be, "Let us *suppress* the confession of our faith," "Let us *put all our weight on top of* the confession of our faith…," or "Let us *put a lid on* the confession of our faith and *hold it down*…." If we aren't determined to really hold fast to the confession of faith, life will try to take our faith away from us.

For example, if you are a believer that is trusting God to place His blessing on your finances, and you're not seeing results, disappointment will try to take the promise of God's provision away from you. Likewise, if you're believing for your body to be healed, but you're not seeing the manifestation of that healing, you may become discouraged and be tempted to let go of the promise of healing.

Understand that whatever God has promised you, the devil will try to pull it out of your hands. The writer of Hebrews was aware of the enemy's tactics, which is why he said, "Hold fast the confession of your faith."

If you're going to see God's promises become a reality, you must stay in your place of faith — you have to say, "No one is going to take this away from me! I'm going to put all my weight on top of God's promise and hold it tightly. I'm not going to let life, the enemy, or anyone else steal from me what God has promised." This is a bulldog determination to never let go of the promise God made to you.

'Confession' Means To Be in Divine Alignment With God

Since we have a better understanding of what it means to *hold fast*, let's look at the next key word in Hebrews 10:23, which the *King James Version* translates as "profession," but would be better translated "confession." It says, "Let us hold fast the profession [confession] of our faith...."

This word "confession" is the Greek word *homologian*, which is a form of the word *homologeo*. The word *homologeo* is a compound of the words *homos* and *logeo*. The word *homos* means *one of the very same kind*, and the word *logeo* means *I say*. When we compound these two words to form *homologian*, it means *to say the same thing*.

Before going further, it's important to note that the word "confession" doesn't quite communicate the fullness of what the Greek word *homologian* really means. For example, let's say you read Rick's book *Dream Thieves*, and after reading it, you agree with what he has written, so much so that you come into full alignment or agreement with his words. What he wrote lines up with what you believe in your heart, hence, your heart beats in sync with his regarding the subject. You are seeing and hearing things the same way, thus, you're in divine alignment with Rick on how to overcome obstacles to fulfill your dreams.

When you apply this understanding to the use of the word *homologian* in Hebrews 10:23, it means that when God has given you a specific promise, you must come into divine alignment with it — a process that often takes time. Sometimes when God gives you a word, you *know* He has spoken to you, but doubt can linger in your soul. Once you recognize that doubt, though, you need to jerk it out and bring yourself into alignment with God. In this divine alignment, you will begin to see and hear the same way God does, and your heart will start to beat in sync with His on this issue. This is the idea behind divine alignment, which, again, takes time and prayer to experience. It requires you to crucify your flesh and renew your mind so that you and God are fully aligned in what He wants to do in your life.

Again, being in divine alignment with God — which is what the Greek word *homologian* describes —is not just parroting His promises with your mouth. It is staying in His Word and in His presence so that your heart and His heart are in full agreement and beat in harmony with each other.

Divine Alignment Also Releases Forgiveness and Healing

The same word *homologian* is used in First John 1:9, which says, "If we confess our sins, he is faithful and just to forgive us our sins, and to cleanse us from all unrighteousness." The word "confess" is a form of the Greek word *homologian*, and its use here tells us that *confessing* sin is not the same as *admitting* sin. The truth is that most people don't confess sin — they just admit their sin.

When you "confess" your sin, it means you and God are getting on the same page about your sin. You're seeing it and hearing it the way God does. How you feel about it and how He feels about it are the same. Your hearts are beating in sync on the issue of sin in your life. When you get into a place of agreement with God like that, that's when your confession becomes powerful and forgiveness is released.

The same can be said of healing. The Bible says, "…By whose stripes ye were healed." When you confess this promise, you're not just saying, "By Jesus' stripes I'm healed." Instead, you and God are on the same page. You have embraced what God says, and you see and hear the subject of healing through Christ how He does. You feel it the way that God feels it, and your heart and His heart are beating in sync together. Thus *confessing* that you are healed by the stripes of Jesus means you are pulled into divine alignment with God regarding healing, and in that position, you can make a confession or a declaration which produces amazing results.

Real Biblical Hope Is a Confident Expectation

Looking again at Hebrews 10:23, it says, "Let us hold fast the profession of our faith…." What is interesting is that when you read this in the Greek text, the word *faith* is not there. Instead, it is the Greek word *elpidos*, which is the word for *hope* or *expectation*.

To be clear, this is not a "hope-so" hope that just hopes something good happens. This word *elpidos* describes biblical hope, which is a hope so real it has turned into *a confident expectation*. It is the picture of a person who is really expecting God's promise to come to pass in his or her life. That's what real hope is. It is a full expectation that what God has told you will absolutely come to pass. In fact, you're waiting for its manifestation right now.

Remember, the writer of Hebrews was writing to Jewish believers who were very discouraged. They had been waiting and waiting to see some good things happen, and because they hadn't seen any results, they were tempted to let go of their faith.

To jolt them out of their negative spiral, the writer said, "*Hold fast* the confession of your faith! Grab hold of it, put all your weight on it, and don't let anyone take it away from you. I'm talking about your *confession*. Get into agreement and on the same page with God, and don't let go of His promise. As you get into divine alignment with Him and what He has promised, cultivate *a full expectation* that what He has promised is exactly what He will do."

Hold On to Your Expectation 'Without Wavering'

To all this, the writer of Hebrews added the words "without wavering." The word "wavering" here is a very interesting term. It is the Greek word *aklines*, which is the word *klines* with an "a" attached to the front. The word *klines* is from the word *klino*, which means *to recline* or *to go to bed*. It describes *one who yields*, *one who surrenders*, or *one who gives up ground or territory*.

When you put an "a" in the front of *klines*, it cancels or reverses the meaning. Hence, the word *aklines* describes *one who doesn't yield*, *one who doesn't surrender*, or *one who doesn't give up ground or territory*. It denotes a person who doesn't lie down or go to bed on their expectation and anticipation of what God has promised.

By using the word *aklines* in Hebrews 10:23, the writer was saying, "Don't you dare do it! Don't you go to bed on your faith! Hold fast to it and embrace tightly the promise God has made to you without wavering!

Hold it down and don't let anyone take it from you. You must get into agreement with God about what He has promised, having a full expectation that He's going to do what He said."

Again, we have to do all these things "without wavering." A person who wavers is one who begins to give up territory and surrender his ground. As time passes and God's promise seems to be delayed, he begins to yield and recline, and eventually he just goes to bed on his faith and give up on his expectation.

Keep in mind, the writer of Hebrews was writing to believers that had been waiting a long time for God's promises to show up in their lives and were tempted to waver (*klines*). They were tempted to *go to bed on their faith*, to surrender and just give up, which is why he said, "Don't do it! Don't waver and let go of your trust in God's word!"

The Reason We Should Never Give Up

The believers to whom the writer of Hebrews was writing may have said, "Why should we keep believing? We've been believing for a long time, and nothing has changed. Why should we keep doing it?" The writer of Hebrews gave them — and us — the reason why they should never give up. He said:

> **...For he is faithful that promised.**
>
> **— Hebrews 10:23**

Friend, if God has made a promise to you, He intends to fully deliver on that promise, but He needs you to get into agreement and alignment with Him. If you are experiencing a delay in receiving what God promised, just look within yourself — the problem might originate with you! Maybe God is ready to answer your question or request. Maybe He's able to give you what you're believing for right now. But for some reason, the spiritual pipeline between you and Him is filled with all kinds of clutter, and the answer can't get through to you.

That's why it's so important for you to understand the word "confession." For God's answers to prayer to make it through to you, you and God have to be in agreement and in alignment. His Word must be in your heart, not just your head. Then out of the abundance of what is in your heart, your mouth will speak His promise, and great things will happen (*see* Matthew 12:34).

If you've been believing and believing for something and haven't seen the manifestation of what you've been believing for, and now you're tempted to forget God's promises and just move on with life, don't give up! Stay in a place of faith because "...He is faithful that promised" (Hebrews 10:23).

The Bible declares, "God is not a man, so he does not lie. He is not human, so he does not change his mind. Has he ever spoken and failed to act? Has he ever promised and not carried it through?" (Numbers 23:19 *NLT*). What God promised to do is exactly what He intends to do. He just needs you to get into agreement and alignment with Him so that manifestation can come into your life.

STUDY QUESTIONS

Study to shew thyself approved unto God, a workman that needeth not to be ashamed, rightly dividing the word of truth.
— 2 Timothy 2:15

1. What new understanding do you have of the Greek word *katecho*? What does the use of this word in Hebrews 10:23 speak to you personally about "holding fast" to your confession of faith?
2. In your own words, describe the meaning of the word "confession" — the Greek word *homologian*. How is this different than just verbally repeating or parroting a verse of Scripture? As you answer, consider the principles echoed in Psalm 119:11; Proverbs 2:1; John 15:7; and James 1:21-25. In light of these verses, is there something you may have missed that you need to begin doing to strengthen your confession of God's Word? If so, what is it?

PRACTICAL APPLICATION

But be ye doers of the word, and not hearers only, deceiving your own selves.
— James 1:22

1. Are you being tempted to let go of a promise from God's Word that you've been holding tightly to for a long time? If so, what is the promise? What is happening in your life that is causing you to want to let go and stop believing? How is this lesson encouraging you to "hold fast"?

2. The "faith" we are instructed to *hold fast* to in Hebrews 10:23 is actually biblical hope — a hope so real it has turned into *a confident expectation*. Our God is the God of all hope (*see* Romans 15:13), and when we put our hope and expectation in Him to do what He has said, He is moved to action! Take time to reflect on this powerful promise in Isaiah 30:18 (*AMPC*):

And therefore the Lord [earnestly] waits [expecting, looking, and longing] to be gracious to you; and therefore He lifts Himself up, that He may have mercy on you and show loving-kindness to you. For the Lord is a God of justice. Blessed (happy, fortunate, to be envied) are all those who [earnestly] wait for Him, who *expect* and look and long for Him [for His victory, His favor, His love, His peace, His joy, and His matchless, unbroken companionship]!

What is the Holy Spirit showing you about expecting good things from God?

LESSON 2

TOPIC

What's Trying To Steal Your Dream?

SCRIPTURES

1. **Hebrews 10:23** — Let us hold fast the profession of our faith without wavering; (for he is faithful that promised).
2. **Proverbs 13:12** — Hope deferred maketh the heart sick....
3. **Hebrews 10:24** — And let us consider one another to provoke unto love and to good works.
4. **Acts 15:39-40** — And the contention was so sharp between them, that they departed asunder one from the other: and so Barnabas took Mark, and sailed unto Cyprus; And Paul chose Silas, and departed, being recommended by the brethren unto the grace of God.
5. **Hebrews 10:25** — Not forsaking the assembling of ourselves together, as the manner of some is; but exhorting one another: and so much the more, as ye see the day approaching.

GREEK WORDS

1. "hold fast" — κατέχω (*katecho*): a compound of the words κατά (*kata*) and ἔχω (*echo*); the word κατά (*kata*) means down, and ἔχω (*echo*) means to have, to hold fast, or to possess; it pictures someone who has something in his possession and is holding it down or suppressing it; as a compound, the new word κατέχω (*katecho*) means to restrain, to hold back, to suppress

2. "profession" — ὁμολογίαν (*homologian*): a compound word derived from the word ὁμολογέω (*homologeo*), which is made up of the words ὁμός (*homos*), which means one of the very same kind, and λογέω (*logeo*), meaning I say; when compounded, ὁμολογίαν (*homologian*) means to say the same thing; to agree

3. "faith" — ἐλπίδος (*elpidos*): derived from the word ἐλπίς (*elpis*), which is the word for hope or expectation; a full expectation that what God has promised will come to pass

4. "without wavering" — ἀκλινῆς (*aklines*): derived from the Greek prefix α (*a*), meaning not or without and has a cancelling effect, and κλίνω (*klino*), which means to recline or to go to bed; it describes one who yields, one who surrenders, one who gives up ground or surrenders territory; when α (*a*) is added to the beginning of κλίνω (*klino*), the new word, ἀκλινής (*aklines*), means do not yield, do not surrender, do not go to bed, do not recline, do not surrender territory

5. "consider" — κατανοέω (*katanoeo*) — a compound of κατα (*kata*) and νοέω (*noeo*); κατα (*kata*) is the word for down, and the word νοέω (*noeo*) means to think; compounded, κατανοέω (*katanoeo*) means to think all the way down; it pictures studying something from top to bottom; to fully contemplate a matter; to consider every point; to observe or understand; not merely a glance or fleeting thought

6. "one another" — ἀλλήλων (*allelon*): describes reciprocal action; one another; each other

7. "provoke" — παροξυσμός (*paroxusmos*): a compound of the words παρα (*para*) and οξυσ (*oxus*); the word παρα (*para*) means alongside, as close as one can get, parallel; the word οξυσ (*oxus*) describes something that is very sharp; the resulting compound, παροξυσμός (*paroxusmos*) describes a person who comes alongside someone else and like a sharp instrument he begins to provoke that person

8. "contention was so sharp" — παροξυσμός (*paroxusmos*): a compound of the words παρα (*para*) and οξυσ (*oxus*); the word παρα (*para*)

means alongside, as close as one can get, parallel; the word οξυσ (*oxus*) describes something that is very sharp; the resulting compound, παροξυσμός (*paroxusmos*) describes a person who comes alongside someone else and like a sharp instrument he begins to provoke that person

SYNOPSIS

Anytime you set out to do something for God or see the fulfillment of a dream that He has placed in your heart, you can be sure there will be challenges and roadblocks along the way. In fact, there are six primary *dream thieves* that will inevitably come and attempt to steal the dream or promise God has given you. In this lesson, we will identify these dream thieves and learn how to keep holding fast to what the Lord has spoken.

The emphasis of this lesson:

The six primary dream thieves that come to steal your dream or promise from God are (1) time; (2) friends; (3) family; (4) the devil; (5) neutrality; and (6) isolation. When you're in isolation, you become more vulnerable to the voice of all these dream thieves.

'Hold Fast' to What God Promised

In Lesson 1, we learned that the book of Hebrews was written to a group of Jewish believers who were very discouraged in their faith. They had been waiting and waiting for some things to happen, but because there were no positive improvements in their situations, they were tempted to give up on what they were believing God to do in their lives.

In Hebrews 10:23, the writer instructed these faith-weary saints with the words, "Let us hold fast the profession of our faith without wavering; (for he is faithful that promised)." We saw that the words "hold fast" in Greek are the word *katecho*, which is a compound of the words *kata* and *echo*. The word *kata* describes *something coming down, conquering,* or *dominating,* and *echo* means *to have, to hold,* and *to possess.*

When these two words are compounded to form *katecho,* it pictures *someone who has something in his possession, and he is holding it down, holding it tightly, and putting all his weight on top of it so no one can take it away from him.* The writer's use of the word *katecho* tells us that in this life, things will come against us to try and take from us what God has promised. To prevent this from happening, we must hold fast to our dream and not let it be stolen.

There Are Six Primary 'Dream Thieves'

Jesus warned us that "the thief comes only to steal and kill and destroy…" (John 10:10 *NIV*). When God plants a word into our hearts, the enemy — and others — will try to take it from us. In fact, Rick identifies six primary *dream thieves* that come to steal God's promise or dream from our lives.

DREAM THIEF NUMBER ONE: **TIME**

The first dream thief that comes against us is the voice of *time*. We're told in Proverbs 13:12, "Hope deferred maketh the heart sick," and that is so true. When you've been believing and waiting for what God promised, the enemy will use the passage of time to gnaw away at your faith. He will speak to you and tell you things like: "If God was going to do this, surely He would have done it by now. Maybe you've been believing wrong, and you didn't hear God correctly. Or maybe you didn't receive a true word from the Lord at all. Maybe you just need to let go of this idea because nothing is happening, and you've been waiting so long." If you listen to this voice, it will steal your dream from you.

DREAM THIEF NUMBER TWO: **FRIENDS**

On top of battling the lies of time, another dream thief will come knocking at your door — your *friends*. Although they love you and are genuinely concerned for you, their perspectives on your choices and what you're believing God for aren't always accurate. As they watch you stand in faith — waiting and believing for weeks, months, or even years — their concern will likely move them to say things like:

> We're really worried about you. Have you seriously thought this through? Have you considered how this dream will impact your livelihood? What about your retirement? What if this opportunity never comes? Maybe it's time to let go and move on.

While their intentions are good, your friends' voices must never supersede the voice of the Holy Spirit. If you listen to them, especially if they're carnal in their thinking, they may talk you out of what God has promised and what you've been waiting for Him to bring about in your life.

DREAM THIEF NUMBER THREE: **FAMILY**

While you are fielding questions and concerns from your friends, you'll also come face to face with dream thief number three — your *family*. Aside from your friends, no one carries a more authoritative voice in your life than your family. And as is almost always the case, your family loves you and wants the very best for you. They care deeply about your well-being, and out of that great concern, they may say things like:

> Are you sure you've heard from God? You've made some mistakes in the past, and stepping out before didn't go well. We realize you've been believing and waiting for this dream to come to pass for quite a while, but maybe it's just not meant to be. Let's face it: You've been stuck in the same place for so long — don't you think it's time to kiss this idea goodbye and move on with your life?

Indeed the voice of your family is powerful, and their input cuts much deeper than most. It is wonderful when you have godly parents and siblings that seek the Lord themselves who will encourage you in your faith. But if you don't have that, and you know you've heard from God, you must choose to hold tightly to His Word and respectfully push aside the voice of your family.

DREAM THIEF NUMBER FOUR: **THE DEVIL**

If you're able to shake the voices of time, friends, and family, there is still another dream thief waiting — one who will use all the others to his advantage. Dream thief number four is the *devil* himself, and he will attack you with sarcasm, condemnation, and mockery, ridiculing you for your faith. He'll whisper things like:

> "You're such a fool! Do you really think you're going to do something for God? You think you'll actually see the manifestation of what you've been believing for all this time? You're nothing but a dreamer on a self-centered 'ego trip.' You've messed up too many times. You're damaged goods, unfit for God's purposes."

The devil would love for you to swallow his accusations. He'd love for you to believe you are nothing more than a prideful dreamer who has no purpose. But he is a liar — the father of lies (*see* John 8:44). Don't believe him!

DREAM THIEF NUMBER FIVE: **NEUTRALITY**

Along with the voices of time, friends, family, and the devil, another more subtle voice will begin to speak to you. This fifth dream thief is *neutrality*. After holding on to God's promise for so long without seeing progress, weariness can set in. In fact, you can become so exhausted and discouraged that you begin to care less about whether the dream happens or not. That's neutrality.

When you become neutral, your fire fades, and your passion for what God placed in your heart begins to dim. If you don't rekindle that flame, you risk losing the dream entirely. That's why you must hold fast to the promise God has given you — no matter how long the wait.

DREAM THIEF NUMBER SIX: **ISOLATION**

Right alongside neutrality — and equally, if not more, damaging — is dream thief number six: *isolation*. Believing for God's promise *alone* is a difficult place to be. That's why we need faith-filled friends who will encourage us, stand with us, and remind us to keep moving forward.

Isolation is dangerous because it causes you to become more vulnerable to the other five dream thieves — time, friends, family, Satan, and neutrality. It leaves you open to doubt, discouragement, and defeat.

But with the empowering strength of God's Spirit living in you, you can stand firm against every accusation and uncertainty these dream thieves bring. Face them head-on with the truth of God's Word and the discernment of the Holy Spirit. As you do, you'll grow stronger, persevere in your calling, and become more and more like Jesus.

'Confessing Your Faith' Is Coming Into Alignment With God

Resisting the dream thieves and facing them head-on is exactly why the writer of Hebrews admonished us to "…hold fast the profession of our faith without wavering…" (Hebrews 10:23). "Hold fast"— the Greek word *katecho* — means you have to *hold, embrace, and wrap your arms around* what God has promised. It means doing everything in your power to put all your weight on top of His divine revelation so no one can take it away from you. This is a determined decision to never let go of what God has promised to you.

Hebrews 10:23 says we are to hold fast to "the *profession* of our faith." We saw that the word "profession" would be better translated as "confession," which is the Greek word *homologian*. It is formed by joining the Greek word *homos* and the word *logeo*. When we compound these two words together to form *homologian*, it describes saying the same thing. However, it's not just repeating or parroting something with our mouths. Rather, it is speaking the same thing, in this case, that God has said, and those words are coming from our *hearts*.

Using the same example from Lesson 1, let's say you read Rick's book *Dream Thieves*, and after reading his words, you agree with what he has written. You hear it, see it, and feel it the same way he does. So much so that you are on the same page with him, and your agreement with him is so strong, it pulls you into full alignment with his words. Finally, your heart begins beating in unison and in sync with his regarding what he has written. That is a picture of the word *homologian* — translated "confession" in Hebrews 10:23.

God wants you to experience this kind of divine alignment with all the promises in His Word. When God speaks His Word to you, rather than just parrot it with your mouth, He wants you to get it deep into your heart. This takes time. You must deal with your flesh and renew your mind. You have to say, "Lord, I'm going to read this and chew on this until my mind is renewed and I begin to see it, hear it, and feel it the same way You do. I want my heart to beat in sync with Yours on this issue." With this attitude of determination, you will become perfectly aligned and on the same page with what God has promised. In that position, you'll become a conduit through which His answers can flow.

Maybe you're in the middle of that process right now. Maybe you've been believing for God to do something for a long time, yet it seems like nothing is happening. But beneath the surface, God has been at work — bringing your soul into alignment with Him.

You've wrestled with unbelief, confronted fret and anxiety, and battled the deafening voices of the dream thieves that are all trying to steal God's promise from you. But through it all, He's been pulling you into alignment with Him. Every day you're becoming more in sync with Him, and soon you'll be like a clear channel — so aligned with His will that His answers can flow freely into your life.

So don't give up! You're in the process and on your way to receiving the manifestation of your dream.

Continue To Expect
What You've Been Expecting

Keep in mind that when the Bible says, "Let us hold fast the profession of our faith," the word *faith* does not appear in the original Greek text — it is actually the Greek word *elpidos*, which is the word for *an expectation*. God wants you to hold on to what you are expecting and to continue to expect it. And He charges you to do this "without wavering" (Hebrews 10:23).

In Greek, the words "without wavering" are a translation of the word *aklines*. The word *klines* — the Greek word for "wavering" — is the term for *a bed* and means *to recline, to yield, to surrender territory*, or *to give up ground*.

However, when an "a" is attached to the front, it cancels the meaning. Hence, the word *aklines* — translated here "without wavering" — means *don't yield, don't surrender, don't recline, don't give up territory, don't surrender any ground*, or *don't go to bed on your faith*.

You might say, "Well, why shouldn't I go to bed on my faith? I've been waiting a long time." The answer to that question is found at the end of Hebrews 10:23. It says, "…For he is faithful that promised." Friend, God is faithful! If He has promised you something, He fully intends to do what He has said.

Let Us 'Consider One Another'

The writer of Hebrews continued his instruction, saying, "And let us consider one another to provoke unto love and to good works" (Hebrews 10:24). The full meaning of the words in this passage are simply marvelous!

Take, for example, the word "consider." It is the Greek word *katanoeo*, a compound of the word *kata* and the word *noeo*. The preposition *kata* means *down* and describes *something moving downward* or *a dominating force*. The word *noeo* is from the word *nous*, which refers to the *mind*, and it means *to think*.

When compounded, the word *katanoeo* means *to think all the way down* or *to study something from the top all the way to the bottom*. It is the idea of *fully contemplating or thoroughly considering a matter.* Rather than just a glance or a brief thought, *katanoeo* — translated here as "consider" — means to really focus on something, thinking it through, pondering it deeply, and looking at every single point. And God says we are to "consider *one another*" (Hebrews 10:23).

The phrase "one another" in Greek is *allelous*, and it describes *reciprocal action.* Here it refers to the members of the Body of Christ, and in context, it means when we see fellow believers, we are to really study them. We are to investigate and ask questions like, "Is he or she struggling in their faith? Are they possibly in a place of isolation or being assaulted by the voices of time, friends, family, or Satan? Are they on the verge of becoming neutral in their faith?"

If you see a fellow Christian experiencing any of these challenges, rather than just taking a glance at them and moving on, you are to really study their condition. Think about it from the top all the way to the bottom. They need you! They need your time, they need your attention, and they need your strength. That is what the phrase "consider one another" really means.

We Are To 'Provoke' One Another to Love and Good Works

Looking again at Hebrews 10:24, the Bible says, "And let us consider one another to provoke unto love and to good works." Notice that the purpose of considering one another is "to provoke unto love and to good works."

The key word here is "provoke." It is a translation of the interesting Greek word *paroxusmos*, a compound of the words *para* and *oxus*. The word *para* means *alongside* or *as close as you can get.* It carries the idea of something that is *parallel.* The word *oxus* describes *something very sharp* or *a very sharp situation.*

When the words *para* and *oxus* are compounded to form the word *paroxusmos*, it describes *someone who has come alongside or parallel to another person for the purpose of sharply prodding and impelling that person to do something.*

Normally *paroxusmos* is a very negative word, which is how we see it used in Acts 15. At that time in Church history, the apostle Paul fell into a very serious disagreement with Barnabas, his friend and traveling companion.

Barnabas wanted to take his nephew, John Mark, along with them on their next missionary trip, but because John Mark had abandoned them during their first trip, Paul didn't want to take him again.

Acts 15:39 and 40 says, "And the contention was so sharp between them, that they departed asunder one from the other: and so Barnabas took Mark, and sailed unto Cyprus; and Paul chose Silas, and departed, being recommended by the brethren unto the grace of God."

Notice at the opening of verse 39, it says that "the contention was so sharp." This phrase is a translation of the Greek word *paroxusmos*. Paul and Barnabus kept coming alongside each other, probably getting in each other's faces, sharply pricking and provoking each other with their words to the point that they had an all-out fight. The contention between them was so sharp and explosive that Paul and Barnabas parted ways.

It's Time We Start
Encouraging Fellow Believers

Reviewing Hebrews 10:24, it says, "And let us consider one another to provoke unto love and to good works." Again, the word "consider" here is the Greek word *katanoeo*. Its use in this verse indicates that God wants us to not just take a glance at fellow believers, but to really study one another. When we see that someone is struggling in his faith and about to give up, we are to study that person and learn what *discourages* and what *encourages* him.

Once we have an idea of what makes this person tick and what he is going through, we are to "provoke" him — *paroxusmos*. We are to come alongside him (*para*) and sharply prod him. But rather than provoke that person to anger and frustration, Hebrews 10:24 says we are to provoke him unto *love* and *good works*.

So when you see a fellow Christian down and dejected, instead of throwing up a quick prayer from a distance, come alongside him or her and say, "Hey, I know you're tempted to give up, but don't do it. Think about what would happen if you give up now. What will become of all the things God has said He wants to do in your life? If you walk away now, you're going to forfeit it all. Hang in there! You're going to make it!" This is what it looks like to come alongside a person and like a sharp instrument, you begin to poke and prod them in a good, right direction.

This "provoking" is especially needed when you sense the dream thieves of time, friends, family, or the devil are speaking to someone, trying to get him or her to quit. Likewise, you are to provoke a person if you see him or her moving into a position of neutrality regarding what God has promised or notice he or she is drawing to a place of isolation. That's when people really need you to take a serious look at them, to come alongside them and say, "I'm not moving away from your side until I've provoked you out of neutrality and isolation and into love and good works."

This practice of encouraging fellow believers is why the writer of Hebrews went on to say, "Not forsaking the assembling of ourselves together, as the manner of some is; but exhorting one another: and so much the more, as ye see the day approaching" (Hebrews 10:25). We will dive deeper into this passage in Lesson 4.

STUDY QUESTIONS

> **Study to shew thyself approved unto God, a workman that needeth not to be ashamed, rightly dividing the word of truth.**
> **— 2 Timothy 2:15**

1. Have you become weary in waiting for God's promise to come to pass in your life? Take time to carefully reflect on what He says in John 15:5-8; Galatians 6:7-9; James 1:12; and Revelation 3:11. What is the Holy Spirit showing you about planting good seed, the process of producing fruit and reaping a harvest, and the need for perseverance?

2. The place of isolation, where you are "doing life" alone, is a dreadful place to be. God has created us to live in relationship with each other. Consider what He says in these passages and identify the life-giving blessings of having godly friends in your life.
    *   Proverbs 13:20
    *   Proverbs 17:17
    *   Proverbs 27:17
    *   Ecclesiastes 4:8-12

PRACTICAL APPLICATION

**But be ye doers of the word, and not hearers only,
deceiving your own selves.
— James 1:22**

1. Of all the dream thieves mentioned, which one(s) has been the most challenging to deal with? Which one(s) are you currently dealing with, and what are they saying to you? Take time to pray: "Holy Spirit, help me. Strengthen me not to waver in faith or let go of Your promises. Please give me the words to say in response to these dream thieves. In Jesus' name. Amen!"

2. Can you think of a time in your own life when someone came alongside you and said things like, "Don't give up now. There's too much on the line. You've already paid too great a price to throw in the towel. Stay in the game! Hold on to what God told you. Trust Him — He's going to come through for you!" How did his or her words encourage you to stay in your place of faith?

LESSON 3

TOPIC

Why Do We Need Each Other?

SCRIPTURES

1. **Hebrews 10:23** — Let us hold fast the profession of our faith without wavering; (for he is faithful that promised).

2. **Romans 1:18** — For the wrath of God is revealed from heaven against all ungodliness and unrighteousness of men, who hold the truth in unrighteousness.

3. **Proverbs 13:12** — Hope deferred maketh the heart sick....

4. **Hebrews 10:24** — And let us consider one another to provoke unto love and to good works.

5. **Acts 15:39** — And the contention was so sharp between them, that they departed asunder one from the other....

6. **Hebrews 10:25** — Not forsaking the assembling of ourselves together, as the manner of some is; but exhorting one another: and so much the more, as ye see the day approaching.

GREEK WORDS

1. "hold fast" — κατέχω (*katecho*): a compound of the words κατά (*kata*) and ἔχω (*echo*); the word κατά (*kata*) means down, and ἔχω (*echo*) means to have, to hold fast, or to possess; it pictures someone who has something in his possession and is holding it down or suppressing it; as a compound, the new word κατέχω (*katecho*) means to restrain, to hold back, to suppress

2. "hold" — κατέχω (*katecho*): a compound of the words κατά (*kata*) and ἔχω (*echo*); the word κατά (*kata*) means down, and ἔχω (*echo*) means to have, to hold fast, or to possess; it pictures someone who has something in his possession and is holding it down or suppressing it; as a compound, the new word κατέχω (*katecho*) means to restrain, to hold back, to suppress

3. "consider" — κατανοέω (*katanoeo*) — a compound of κατα (*kata*) and νοέω (*noeo*); κατα (*kata*) is the word for down, and the word νοέω (*noeo*) means to think; compounded, κατανοέω (*katanoeo*) means to think all the way down; it pictures studying something from top to bottom; to fully contemplate a matter; to consider every point; to observe, understand; not merely a glance or fleeting thought

4. "one another" — ἀλλήλων (*allelon*): describes reciprocal action; one another; each other

5. "provoke" — παροξυσμός (*paroxusmos*): a compound of the words παρα (*para*) and οξυσ (*oxus*); the word παρα (*para*) means alongside, as close as one can get, parallel; the word οξυσ (*oxus*) describes something that is very sharp; the resulting compound, παροξυσμός (*paroxusmos*) describes a person who comes alongside someone else and like a sharp instrument he begins to provoke that person

6. "contention was so sharp" — παροξυσμός (*paroxusmos*): a compound of the words παρα (*para*) and οξυσ (*oxus*); the word παρα (*para*) means alongside, as close as one can get, parallel; the word οξυσ (*oxus*) describes something that is very sharp; the resulting compound, παροξυσμός (*paroxusmos*) describes a person who comes alongside someone else and like a sharp instrument he begins to provoke that person

SYNOPSIS

It is very common for the enemy to attack when you're in a place of faith, trying to do what God has called you to do. The devil knows if you stay in that place and if you stand in faith for what you believe God has promised, you're going to receive God's promise, and people's lives are going to be changed. Satan doesn't want that to happen, which is why he tries to move you out of your place of faith.

Rick shared how he and his wife, Denise, can personally testify that over their years of ministry, God has asked them and their family to tackle some pretty impossible tasks — such as building a new television studio in Moscow. But they've learned that if they remain in a place of faith, they can do anything God asks of them, and the same holds true for you.

As you stand in faith, holding tenaciously to God's Word, you will receive what He has promised and accomplish what He has called you to do, despite the enemy's threats and attacks.

The emphasis of this lesson:

It is difficult to stay in a place of faith when you're by yourself. You need like-minded people around you who can encourage you and provoke you to not give up and to hold fast to your faith until you receive the manifestation of what you've been believing to come to pass in your life.

Don't Let Go of What God Promised

Before we dive deep into Lesson 3, let's quickly review a few of the things we have learned so far. In Hebrews 10:23, the Bible says, "Let us hold fast the profession of our faith without wavering; (for he is faithful that promised)."

We have seen that in the original Greek text the words "hold fast" are translated from a form of the word *katecho*, which is a compound of the word *kata* and the word *echo*. The word *kata* means *down* and often describes *something conquering or dominating*, and the word *echo* means *to have, to hold, to possess*, or *to embrace*. When these words are joined to form *katecho*, it means *to have, hold, or possess something and to embrace it or hold it down so tightly that it can't get away.*

The idea in this verse is that when God has promised you something, He wants you to "hold fast" to it. This is an internal determination and a verbal declaration that says, "God gave me this, and I'm going to hold it, embrace it, and possess it with all my might. In fact, I'm putting all my weight on top of it, and I'm not letting life, the devil, or anyone else take it away from me."

This word *katecho* can also be used in a negative sense, which is what we see in Romans 1:18. Here, Paul wrote, "For the wrath of God is revealed from heaven against all ungodliness and unrighteousness of men, who *hold* the truth in unrighteousness." The word "hold" in this verse is *katecho*, and here it pictures ungodly men who have heard and know the truth, but they don't like it. Consequently, they suppress the truth — they hold it, sit on it, and put a tight lid on it so it can't get out and bring people freedom.

In a positive sense, when God makes a promise to you in His Word or by His Spirit, He commands you to wrap your arms around it, put all your weight on top of it, and hang on to it so tightly that no one and nothing can take it away. Remember, "…He is faithful that promised" (Hebrews 10:23), which means God intends to do exactly what He said He would do.

Stand Against These Six 'Dream Thieves'

In Lesson 2, we identified six primary *dream thieves* that come to steal the dream or promise God has given us. If they succeed in their efforts, they will steal our individual purpose in the marvelous plan of God, which would be quite tragic. Here is a quick review of each one:

Dream Thief #1: *Time*. We are told in Proverbs 13:12, "Hope deferred maketh the heart sick…." When the promise of God seems to be delayed in becoming a reality, the enemy will use the passage of time to speak to you and attempt to chip away at your faith, saying things like: "This thing is never going to happen. You've been waiting and waiting, and there is no sign of any change on the horizon. Maybe you ought to just let it go."

When you begin to hear these kinds of doubts, that's when you need to "hold fast" even more tightly to what God spoke to you. It will come to pass "in due time" (*see* 1 Peter 5:6).

Dream Thief #2: *Friends*. Along with the voice of time, you'll also face the voice of your *friends*. While they love you and are concerned about you, their view of your situation may not always be correct. When they see you waiting for something for a long time and still nothing is happening, they may try to talk you out of it.

"We know you love God and want to do His will," they may say. "But maybe you're wrong about this. Maybe what you are believing for is not really what God intended. Maybe you misunderstood and confused your feelings for the voice of God."

If you listen to those friends' voices, they will take God's promise and the dream He gave you right out of your hands — even if they meant well. So when you hear this line of questioning, you need to "hold fast" to what God spoke to you, embracing it more tightly than ever.

Dream Thief #3: *Family.* In addition to the voice of time and your friends, there is a third dream thief — your *family.* Family can have such a big influence in your life, and unlike friends you can't always walk away from them. Those in your family are with you for life. Hence, this dream thief is a much more personal one to navigate.

Certainly, your family loves you and is legitimately concerned about your welfare. But out of true concern, when they see that your life is on pause and that you're waiting and waiting yet nothing is happening, they may say, "Why don't you just let go of this idea and move on with life. We know you are devoted to God, but what you have been waiting to see happen may just be a fantasy. You're dreaming, and we are very concerned for your future."

Indeed your family's voice can be very authoritative, so when you hear these kinds of statements, you need to really "hold fast" to what God has told you. You must be determined to embrace it tightly, put all your spiritual weight on it, and hold it down with the strength of the Holy Spirit.

Dream Thief #4: *The Devil.* The fourth dream thief is *Satan* himself. He will try to convince you that the grand and glorious dream you've been holding on to is just your own self-exalting fantasy and that God's real plan for your life is more "humble" in nature. (What Satan really means is that God's plan for you is "a more obscure and meaningless task," which again is not true!)

When the enemy whispers his lies and mocks you, calling you ridiculous, foolish, and a mere dreamer, open your mouth and confront him head-on. Declare aloud what you have heard from God and that you will *not* budge or be moved from God's plan!

Dream Thief #5: *Neutrality*. If you make it beyond the voice of time, your friends, your family, and the devil himself, you will run into dream thief number five, which is *neutrality*. This is a real serious enemy that shows up when you grow weary of waiting. You become so tired of believing for God to come through for you that you no longer care whether His promise happens or not.

I've waited and believed for a long time, you think to yourself. *And I used to think this was so important, but it never happened. Now, I'm just exhausted, depleted, and worn out, and I really don't care if it happens or not.* That is what neutrality sounds like. If that's where you are, it's time for you to dig in your spiritual heels, wrap your arms tightly around what God has promised, and ask the Holy Spirit to reignite your passion for what He has called you to do.

Dream Thief #6: *Isolation*. There's one more dream thief, and it is called *isolation*. When you are in a position of isolation, you are more vulnerable to the assaults of all the other dream thieves — time, friends, family, the devil, and neutrality. That is why it is vital that you learn not to do life alone but to walk the walk of faith with others.

Friend, God never intended you to live in isolation. You were created to live in relationships with others as a vital part of His Church. Of course, there are many Christians who attend a local church, but they are still lonely because they live isolated from the people around them. For various reasons, they tend to arrive late and leave as soon as the service is over, never taking the time to purposely talk and connect with others.

If that describes you — or you have been attending a church in which you can't seem to connect with the people — pray and ask the Holy Spirit to help you find a local church where you can connect with people who have the same precious faith. When the dream thieves come around, those in your church family will encourage you to stay in a place of faith.

Become an Avid Student of Those You Do Life With

As a part of a vibrant fellowship of believers, we can be encouraged and can encourage others. It is important not to be isolated from each other. This is why Hebrews 10:24 says, "And let us consider one another to provoke unto love and to good works." There are three very important words in this passage that we began looking at in Lesson 2, the first of which is the word "consider."

In Greek, the word "consider" is *katanoeo*, a compound of the words *kata* and *noeo*. The preposition *kata* means *down*, and the word *noeo* means *to think*. When these words are compounded, a literal translation of the word *katanoeo* would be *to think down*. It describes *deep contemplation*. Rather than just a passing thought or a quick glance, the word *katanoeo* means *to think something through from the top to the bottom*. It is the idea of thinking long and hard about something.

What are we to deeply ponder and thoroughly consider? The Bible says "one another," which is a translation of the Greek word *allelous*, a form of *allelon*. This word describes *something reciprocal*, and here, it denotes *reciprocal relationships* in the Body of Christ.

The use of this word *allelon* means we need to have people in our life that we are "considering," and we also need people that are "considering" us. Again, to "consider" — the Greek word *katanoeo* — indicates we need to be focused on and studying believers who are around us, and we need other believers focused on and studying us.

To be clear, this includes becoming an avid student of your spouse, your children, and your friends. It means learning what encourages them, what discourages them, and really thinking about them from the top all the way to the bottom — just like you would study a subject in school. Moreover, this "considering" should be a reciprocal, mutual practice. We were not meant to live in isolation but in a community as a part of one another's lives.

God Wants Us To Poke and Prod Others in a Positive Way

Hebrews 10:24 says that we are specifically to consider one another "…to *provoke* unto love and to good works." We learned that the word "provoke" is a translation of the Greek word *paroxusmos*, a compound of the words *para* and *oxus*.

The word *para* describes *something that is parallel* or *side-by-side*. It carries the idea being close. And the word *oxus* describes *something sharp* or *a very sharp situation*. When we compound *para* and *oxus* to create the word *paroxusmos*, it *depicts someone who comes alongside someone else with a sharp instrument,* such as a poker or a sharp stick, *to poke and prick him until he gets agitated.*

One of the best examples of this is in Acts 15:39 where the Bible tells us that Paul and Barnabas had fallen into a fierce disagreement over whether or not to take John Mark, Barnabas' nephew, along with them on their next missionary journey. Scripture says, "And the contention was so sharp between them, that they departed asunder one from the other..." (Acts 15:39).

The phrase "contention was so sharp" is the Greek word *paroxusmos.* In this case, it carries a negative connotation. Paul and Barnabas were so upset that they came alongside each other and began to poke and prod one another so sharply that they eventually parted ways.

With the same intensity that these men provoked each other into a heated fight, Hebrews 10:24 says we are to provoke one another "...unto love and to good works." What does this look like? Rick gave the following example of how his wife, Denise, served to provoke him in a positive way:

> The very first time I ever taught on Hebrews 10:23, which was many years ago, I was very excited about teaching it, but after I was done, I felt that I had failed to communicate it clearly. When we walked out of church and got into the car, I told Denise, 'Oh, I really failed today. I wanted to communicate this truth, but I feel like I didn't hit the target or get to where I wanted to go.'
>
> Denise said, 'Rick, what are you talking about?'
>
> In that moment, she came close alongside me and said, 'What you said was so good, and I'm very encouraged! You encouraged the people to have reciprocal relationships with each other. You made it clear that we are to come alongside other people to provoke them — not to conflict, but to do what is good and to stay in a place of faith.'
>
> 'Oh, Denise!' I answered with a smile. 'I know what you're doing. You're doing what I just preached! You're coming alongside me and you're sharply provoking me.'
>
> Suddenly, it dawned on me, *I guess I did a better job than I thought because Denise is certainly practicing what I just preached!*

Just like Denise came alongside Rick and encouraged him, we should come along others around us and "provoke" them to love and good works!

Who Do You Know That Is About To Give Up?

Can you think of someone who was once in a place of strong faith, but now he is thinking about letting go of it and God's promise to him? Maybe the dream thieves of time, friends, family, and the devil have been talking to him during the waiting season. Each of these dream thieves will try to get him to give up and walk away from what he's been believing God for. He may have become tired and moved into a neutral position where he no longer cares about what he was believing God to do. He may even be in a place of isolation where he is all alone and losing the fight to stay in his place of faith.

That is the person the Holy Spirit wants you to "consider." He wants you to look at others and really study them from the top to the bottom until you understand their situation and know what you need to do to help them. Take some time to contemplate and learn what encourages them and what practical steps you can take to bring some joy to their life.

Once the Holy Spirit makes things clear, come alongside those people and begin to "provoke" them in a positive direction. Begin to say, "You can do it! You've waited too long and are too close to victory to give up now. Don't walk away from the promise God has for you because you're right on the edge of your breakthrough! You've been standing in faith and believing God to come through, and people are watching you. Do you want them to see a failed picture of faith or a victorious one?"

This is a picture of what it means to provoke someone unto love and good works — and one of the good works is holding fast to what God has promised.

In our next lesson, we will take a look at Hebrews 10:25, where the writer says, "Not forsaking the assembling of ourselves together, as the manner of some is; but exhorting one another: and so much the more, as ye see the day approaching."

STUDY QUESTIONS

**Study to shew thyself approved unto God, a workman that
needeth not to be ashamed, rightly dividing the word of truth.
— 2 Timothy 2:15**

1. As you finish reading this lesson, what is your greatest takeaway that the Holy Spirit is showing you about your need for having other believers in your life?
2. What does Hebrews 10:24, which instructs us to "consider one another," have in common with First Thessalonians 5:11 and Romans 14:19 and 15:2?

PRACTICAL APPLICATION

**But be ye doers of the word, and not hearers only,
deceiving your own selves.
— James 1:22**

When you're in a position of *isolation*, you are more vulnerable to the attacks of all the dream thieves. That is why it is vital for you to learn not to do life alone but to walk the walk of faith with others.

1. Who are you "doing life" with right now? Who do you consider your closest friend(s)?
2. When something wonderful and exciting happens, who are the people you can't wait to tell?
3. When an emergency arises, who do you know you can count on and reach out to for help?
4. If you don't really have solid answers to these questions, *pray* and ask the Holy Spirit to help you develop healthy friendships. Ask Him to lead you to the people He knows will be the best fit for you to be in relationship with and vice versa.

TOPIC

Are You Close to Your Harvest?

SCRIPTURES

1. **Hebrews 10:23** — Let us hold fast the profession of our faith without wavering; (for he is faithful that promised).

2. **Hebrews 10:24** — And let us consider one another to provoke unto love and to good works.

3. **Hebrews 10:25** — Not forsaking the assembling of ourselves together, as the manner of some is; but exhorting one another: and so much the more, as ye see the day approaching.

4. **Acts 15:39** — And the contention was so sharp between them, that they departed asunder one from the other: and so Barnabas took Mark, and sailed unto Cyprus.

5. **Galatians 6:9** — And let us not be weary in well doing: for in due season we shall reap, if we faint not.

6. **Luke 3:16** — …One mightier than I cometh, the latchet of whose shoes I am not worthy to unloose.…

GREEK WORDS

1. "consider" — **κατανοέω** (*katanoeo*) — a compound of **κατα** (*kata*) and **νοέω** (*noeo*); **κατα** (*kata*) is the word for down, and the word **νοέω** (*noeo*) means to think; compounded, **κατανοέω** (*katanoeo*) means to think all the way down; it pictures studying something from top to bottom; to fully contemplate a matter; to consider every point; to observe, understand; not merely a glance or fleeting thought

2. "one another" — **ἀλλήλων** (*allelon*): describes reciprocal action; one another; each other

3. "provoke" — **παροξυσμός** (*paroxusmos*): a compound of the words **παρα** (*para*) and **οξυσ** (*oxus*); the word **παρα** (*para*) means alongside, as close as one can get, parallel; the word **οξυσ** (*oxus*) describes something that is very sharp; the resulting compound, **παροξυσμός** (*paroxusmos*) describes a person who comes alongside someone else and like a sharp instrument he begins to provoke that person

4. "not forsaking" — ἐγκαταλείπω (*egkataleipo*): a triple compound made up of the preposition ἐν (*en*), meaning in, and the words κατα (*kata*) and λείπω (*leipo*); kata means down, and λείπω (*leipo*) is to be far behind; compounded, ἐγκαταλείπω (*egkataleipo*) can mean to abandon or leave behind; it can also picture someone who feels down, behind, or discouraged

5. "faint not" — ἐκλύω (*ekluo*): a combination of ἐκ (*ek*), meaning out, and λύω (*luo*) which depicts something that becomes so loosened that it simply falls off; the compound ἐκλύω (*ekluo*) depicts a person who has been waiting so long that he finally gives up, gives out, and surrenders

6. "unloose" — λύω (*luo*): depicts something that becomes so loosened that it simply falls off

7. "exhorting" — παρακαλέω (*parakaleo*): a compound of the words παρα (*para*) and καλέω (*kaleo*); the word παρα (*para*) means alongside, as close as one can get, parallel; the word καλέω (*kaleo*) means to call; it describes one who calls out, beckons, or speaks; compounded, the new word παρακαλέω (*parakaleo*) describes one who comes alongside and speaks; this is the root word in παράκλητος (*parakletos*), which is translated Comforter in reference to the Holy Spirit; παρακαλέω (*parakaleo*) was used in a military sense to depict a commanding officer who comes alongside his troops before a battle and stir them to action with encouraging words

SYNOPSIS

In the First Century, there was a group of Jewish believers that had become very discouraged in their faith. They had been waiting and waiting for things God had promised, but nothing was changing. Consequently, they were tempted to think that they had been mistaken in what they were believing God for — that it was just a mere fantasy that was never really going to happen.

It was to these downtrodden believers that the writer of Hebrews said, "Let us hold fast the profession of our faith without wavering..." (Hebrews 10:23). In other words, he urged them to hold on to what God had promised them with all their might and not let it go. Why? Because "...He is faithful that promised" (Hebrews 10:23).

What has God pledged to you? Has He promised His healing? Has He pledged to bring order and blessing to your finances? Has He prophesied to restore your relationship with your spouse or bring your wayward child back into relationship with Him? Has He spoken to you about a new job or career opportunity? Whatever God has pledged to you, wrap your arms around it and hold fast to it without wavering. God is faithful! He will bring to pass what He promised!

The emphasis of this lesson:

If God has promised you something, He will be faithful to bring it to pass. You will reap the harvest you are believing Him to provide if you don't give up, and it will happen in due season. Your job is to stay in a place of faith until you receive it and help others do the same.

We Need 'Reciprocal Relationships'

Immediately after telling believers to hold fast their confession of faith, the writer of Hebrews went on to encourage them, saying:

> **And let us consider one another to provoke unto love and to good works: Not forsaking the assembling of ourselves together, as the manner of some is; but exhorting one another: and so much the more, as ye see the day approaching.**
> **— Hebrews 10:24-25**

Before we unpack the rich meaning of verse 25, let's briefly review the truths we have learned in Hebrews 10:24, which we have seen from the previous lessons is describing *reciprocal relationships*.

"Consider one another." The word "consider" is the Greek word *katanoeo*. We have covered the meaning of this word before, but because it's so vital, let's go a little deeper so we really grasp what God is saying.

The first part of the word is *kata*, which means *down*. The second part of the word is *noeo*, which means *to think*. When these two words are compounded to form *katanoeo*, it means *to deeply contemplate, to study, to examine*, or *to observe*.

What are we supposed to observe? Hebrews 10:24 says "one another." In Greek, this is the word *allelous*, which comes from the word *allelon* and describes *one another* or *a reciprocal relationship*. If we just stopped here, we'd have a profound message by itself. First, it says we are to consider one another, and we're to do it *reciprocally*. This is not just what we do for someone else. We need someone else to do this for us.

What do we need to do to others, and what do we need others to do for us? We need to deeply contemplate others, and we need other people to deeply contemplate us. This means really studying someone and having someone else really study us. The word *katanoeo* also means examining or observing someone else and having someone else deeply examine or observe us.

That is what *katanoeo* means. Someone observes us from the top all the way to the bottom, examining every part of what encourages us and what discourages us, and vice versa. All of us need people in our life to help us stay in our place of faith. Again, the words "one another" are the Greek word *allelon*, which means considering one another in a *reciprocal* manner.

Who does this for you? Hopefully your spouse does this, if you have a spouse. Or maybe it's your children, a sibling, or a friend. Rick shared that he has some very close relationships with people he stays in touch with every day. He believes they need his voice and he needs their voice to *katanoeo* — consider each other deeply. He contemplates them deeply, studying them, examining them, and observing them because he wants them to do what God has called them to do. And they contemplate Rick in the same way.

They have each taken the time to learn what encourages each other and how to recognize when they are in need of encouragement. Just like they need Rick's voice, Rick needs their voice. In the same way he considers and encourages them daily, they reciprocate and provide similar input in his life.

Indeed there is great, mutual benefit by being in relationship with people in the Body of Christ. That's why you need to be in a local church where you can have this kind of reciprocal fellowship and attention. If you're not in a place where you are experiencing this, then reach out to us at RENNER Ministries. We would love to pray for you and really encourage you in your faith.

We Are Called To 'Provoke' One Another in a Positive Way

Looking again at Hebrews 10:24, it says, "And let us consider one another to provoke unto love and to good works." We've seen in our two previous lessons that the word "provoke" is the Greek word *paroxusmos*, which is normally a very negative word. It is a compound of the words *para* and *oxus*. The word *para* means *to be parallel or alongside something or someone*. The word *oxus* describes *something very sharp* like a poker or a sharpened stick.

When *para* and *oxus* are compounded to form *paroxusmos*, it means *to come up alongside someone else and repeatedly poke him or her until he or she is finally provoked into action*. We've noted that the best example of this is in Acts 15:39 where we find that the apostle Paul and his friend and fellow traveler Barnabas provoked each other in a negative way. Paul was upset with Barnabas because Barnabas wanted to take his nephew John Mark with them on their second missionary trip. However, because John Mark had abandoned them on their first missionary journey, Paul thought John Mark was too young and immature to go with them.

Exactly what they said and did to each other we do not know. But what resulted is written in Acts 15:39, which says, "And *the contention was so sharp* between them, that they departed asunder one from the other...." The phrase "the contention was so sharp" is a translation of the Greek word *paroxusmos*, which tells us that Barnabas and Paul came alongside each other, and they began to poke and prick one another until finally the words they exchanged with each other were so sharp that they went their separate ways.

This same word — *paroxusmos* — is used in Hebrews 10:24, but in a positive sense. It is translated as the word "provoke," and it means that after we have deeply observed, studied, and examined a fellow believer, we are to come alongside them and provoke them to stay in their place of faith. And they are to do the same for us, as these actions are to be reciprocal.

Here is what this might sound like:

> Don't give up! You may be tired, but you can't quit now. I know you've waited and waited, but you've invested too much time believing God for your breakthrough. You're not going to give

up your place of faith. No! You've already declared your faith and told others what God is going to do, so hold on. In fact, I'm going to stand in faith with you until you see God's promise become a reality.

This is what we're called to do to one another. We are called by God to poke, prod, and prick one another until we finally bring each other to a place where we say, "Okay, okay! I'm not going to give up — I'm going to stay in my place of faith!" This is what it means to "...provoke unto love and to good works" (Hebrews 10:24). You need to be doing this for someone, and someone needs to be doing this for you.

What Does the Word 'Forsaking' Mean?

Along with considering one another and provoking one another in a positive way to love and good works, the writer of Hebrews takes his instruction further in Hebrews 10:25, telling us:

> **Not forsaking the assembling of ourselves together, as the manner of some is; but exhorting one another: and so much the more, as ye see the day approaching.**

Notice the word "forsaking" at the start of the verse. It is a form of the Greek word *egkataleipo*, which is a triple compound of three words: *en*, *kata*, and *leipo*. The word *en* means *in*, the word *kata* means *down*, and the word *leipo* means *far behind* or *to be lacking*. When these three words are compounded to form the word *egkataleipo*, it describes *a person who is in a state of feeling down and out and far behind others*.

Without question, a person who is "forsaking" assembling together with other Christians is one who is discouraged, depressed, and feels like everyone else has *surpassed* him. We might even say he feels *outside the circle of his group*. In this condition of feeling *defeated* and *far behind others* in his spiritual life or in his life in general, the last place he wants to be is in church. He doesn't want to hear about all the things God is doing in the lives of others — how they are receiving from God and being used by Him.

These people might lament: "I'm just feeling so down and so far behind everyone else. I don't want to hear people shouting and praising God, and

I don't want anyone speaking positive words of encouragement to me. I just want to be left alone."

Have you been there and done that? Ironically, the moment you least want someone to provoke you in a positive way is the moment you need it most. When you're feeling down and out, it's not the time to give up — it's the time to press in closer to God and closer to His people. That is what the writer of Hebrews meant when he said, "Not forsaking."

We Must Do Our Best To 'Faint Not'

Knowing our human tendency to want to quit when things get tough and when we're drained of our strength, the Holy Spirit moved on the apostle Paul to issue this vital charge in Galatians 6:9:

> **And let us not be weary in well doing: for in due season we shall reap, if we faint not.**

The place of "well-doing" is the place of faith. Thus God says we are not to grow weary in our place of faith. Although we may get tired from waiting and waiting for God's promise to come to pass, we mustn't give in to the temptation to quit. Instead, we need to hold fast to the confession of our faith. If we have planted good seed in faith, we are going to reap a good harvest. We have God's Word on it: "…For in due season *we shall reap*, if we faint not" (Galatians 6:9).

What is interesting is that the words "faint not" in Greek are a form of the word *ekluo*, a compound of the words *ek* and *luo*. The word *ek* means *out*, and the word *luo* means *to loosen* or *to relax*. An example of the word *luo* is found in Luke 3:16, where John the Baptist said he was not worthy to *unloose* Jesus' shoes. The word "unloose" is the Greek word *luo*. The word *luo* depicts shoes with all the strands becoming so loosened that they can no longer be held to a person's feet and they just fall off.

When we compound the words *ek* and *luo* to form *ekluo* — translated as "faint not" in Galatians 6:9 — it describes *a person who's just so undone* because he's been waiting for so long that he gives up and gives out. He surrenders and walks away from what he was believing God to provide, forfeiting the desired harvest. Pressures that have come against him have unraveled him, causing him to loosen his grip until the answer slips from his hands, and the harvest is lost.

Impatience Can Cause Us To Lose Our Harvest

Rick shared this personal story, illustrating what it means to "faint" after becoming weary in well-doing during a time of waiting.

> When I was a teenager, I decided I was going to grow some corn on the side of my daddy's garage. At the time, I knew nothing about farming, but I liked corn. So I bought some corn seeds and went out to the side of Daddy's garage, and I began to plant my corn in a nice, neat, orderly row. I can't tell you how excited I was.
>
> The next day, I went out to see if anything was poking up through the soil, but there was nothing. Two, three, four, and five days in a row I went outside to look for growth, but each time I went, I saw nothing. I kept thinking, *Where is the corn? I put seeds in the ground, but I see no stalks beginning to grow.*
>
> Finally, one day I said, 'You know, I really ought to be seeing some action by now. There must be something defective with this seed.'
>
> Frustrated, I got a little spatula from the kitchen, and I began to dig up all my seed. To my amazement, I discovered that all the seeds I had planted were sprouting roots and were just about to poke up through the soil. Unfortunately, because of my impatience, I aborted my harvest. That is why the Bible says, 'And let us not be weary in well doing: for in due season we shall reap, if we faint not' (Galatians 6:9).

Friend, the same holds true for you! You *will* reap a harvest of what you are believing God for if you don't give up. It will happen in due season. If He has pledged something to you, He fully intends to fulfill His promise!

So if you're feeling down, left out, and lagging far behind other Christians, don't give in to those emotions. This is not the time for you to fall out of fellowship with other believers. Instead of giving in to your emotions and avoiding the reciprocal encouragement that you need, Hebrews 10:25 says we are to be "…exhorting one another: and so much the more, as ye see the day approaching."

God Wants Us To 'Exhort One Another'

Instead of forsaking the assembling of ourselves together, we are called to "exhort one another." The word "exhorting," which appears in Hebrews 10:25, is the Greek word *parakaleo*, a compound of the words *para* and *kaleo*. As we've seen, the word *para* describes *something that is parallel* or *alongside*, and the word *kaleo* means *to call, to beckon*, or *to speak to someone*. When you compound the two words to form *parakaleo*, it describes *someone who comes alongside someone else and begins to call out, urge, beg, and beseech that person to make a correct decision.*

What's interesting is that *parakaleo* is the root for the word *Parakletos*, which is translated as *Comforter* in John 14, 15, and 16. The Comforter is the Holy Spirit who walks alongside us to encourage us, direct us, correct us, counsel us, and urge us to stay in the fight. This lets us know that when we come alongside other believers to encourage them to stay in faith, we are ministering to them in a very similar way that the Holy Spirit ministers to us.

When you see someone who's about to walk away from their place of faith and they've fallen out of fellowship with other believers, rather than just think, *I wonder what happened to so and so*, you need to find that person. You need to get on the phone, knock on their door, send them an email or a text and say: "Hey, you need to be in church with people who love and care about you. Even if you feel down, out, and far behind everyone else, don't give into your emotions and quit. You are right on the edge of receiving what you've been believing. So stay in your place of faith!"

Friend, we need this kind of candid encouragement in our lives, provoking us to love and good works. The Bible clearly states in Galatians 6:9, "…We shall reap, if we faint not." So don't give up! Your harvest — the promise you've been waiting for — is right in front of you. If God has made a pledge to you, you can trust Him to keep it. Your job is to stay in a place of faith until you receive the manifestation of what you're believing for and encourage others to do the same.

STUDY QUESTIONS

Study to shew thyself approved unto God, a workman that needeth not to be ashamed, rightly dividing the word of truth.
— 2 Timothy 2:15

1. When Hebrews 10:24 says we are to "consider one another," it means we are to deeply ponder and study each other, which includes fellow believers as well as our families, spouses, and children. To help you

become a better student of your family, spouse, and kids, take time to answer these questions (if you don't know the answers, look for opportunities to observe them and ask them questions).

- Name three things that your *spouse* loves and one thing he or she really dislikes.
- Name three things that each of your *children* love and one thing they can't stand.
- What are two things that *encourage* your spouse? How about your children?
- What kind of things *discourage* your spouse? How about your children?

2. Four times Jesus called the Holy Spirit the "Comforter," which in Greek is *Parakletos*. God has called Him to walk alongside you and call out to you as a voice of encouragement, counsel, direction, and correction. Take time to reflect on Jesus' words about the Holy Spirit in John 14:16-17, 26; 15:26; and 16:7, 13-15. In your own words, write what roles He plays in your life.

PRACTICAL APPLICATION

But be ye doers of the word, and not hearers only, deceiving your own selves. —James 1:22

1. Believe it or not, *you* are an answer to someone's prayers. Right now, someone you know is struggling to stay in his place of faith. You may already know who it is because you have thought of this person frequently over the past several days. Take time now to pray for him and then reach out to him by phone, text, or in person to give him a word of encouragement.

2. Recall a time (or two) in your life when you were weary from waiting and tempted to give up on God's promise just before it manifested. As you remember the details of what happened, take time to *thank God* that you didn't quit believing just before the blessing came.

TOPIC

Is the Enemy Fighting Your Light?

SCRIPTURES

1. **Hebrews 10:23** — Let us hold fast the profession of our faith without wavering; (for he is faithful that promised).
2. **Hebrews 10:25** — Not forsaking the assembling of ourselves together, as the manner of some is; but exhorting one another: and so much the more, as ye see the day approaching.
3. **Hebrews 10:32** — But call to remembrance the former days, in which, after ye were illuminated, ye endured a great fight of afflictions.

GREEK WORDS

1. "hold fast" — **κατέχω** (*katecho*): a compound of the words **κατά** (*kata*) and **ἔχω** (*echo*); the word **κατά** (*kata*) means down, and **ἔχω** (*echo*) means to have, to hold fast, or to possess; it pictures someone who has something in his possession and is holding it down or suppressing it; as a compound, the new word **κατέχω** (*katecho*) means to restrain, to hold back, to suppress
2. "not forsaking" — **ἐγκαταλείπω** (*egkataleipo*): a triple compound made up of the preposition **ἐν** (*en*), meaning in, and the words **κατα** (*kata*) and **λείπω** (*leipo*); kata means down, and **λείπω** (*leipo*) is to be far behind; the resulting compound **ἐγκαταλείπω** (*egkataleipo*) can mean to abandon or leave behind; it can also picture someone who feels down, behind, or discouraged
3. "manner" — **ἔθος** (*ethos*): a behavior, a habit, or a custom
4. "exhorting" — **παρακαλέω** (*parakaleo*): a compound of the words **παρα** (*para*) and **καλέω** (*kaleo*); the word **παρα** (*para*) means alongside, as close as one can get, parallel; the word **καλέω** (*kaleo*) means to call; it describes one who calls out, beckons, or speaks; compounded, the new word **παρακαλέω** (*parakaleo*) describes one who comes alongside and speaks; this is the root word in **παράκλητος** (*parakletos*), which is translated Comforter in reference to the Holy Spirit; **παρακαλέω** (*parakaleo*) was used in a military sense to depict a commanding officer

who comes alongside his troops before a battle and stirs them to action
with encouraging words

5. "call to remembrance" — ἀναμιμνήσκω (*anamimnesko*): made up of
the prefix ἀνα (*ana*), which means to do it again and carries the idea
of upward movement, and the word μνεία (*mneia*), which is the word
for a statue, monument, or memorial; the word μνεία (*mneia*) is also
the word for a grave

6. "illuminated" — φωτίζω (*photidzo*): where we get the English word
for photograph; a brilliant flash of light that leaves a permanent and
lasting impression

SYNOPSIS

Have you been waiting a long, long time for the promise of God to come
to pass in your life? Has the delay in seeing your dream become a reality
tempted you to give up and walk away from what you have been believing?
That is exactly where the Jewish believers were when they received the
letter we have come to know as the book of Hebrews.

To these discouraged Christians — and to us who are dealing with discouragement today — the writer of Hebrews said, "But call to remembrance
the former days, in which, after ye were illuminated..." (Hebrews 10:32). In
this lesson, we will learn what this verse means and discover the power of
remembering the good things God has done.

The emphasis of this lesson:

**Instead of skipping church when we're discouraged, we need to get
around other faith-filled believers and allow them to encourage us and
for us to encourage them when they're in need. We are to call to remembrance and never forget all the good things God has done — especially
the moments He illuminated our hearts with truth.**

A Review of Our Anchor Verse

As we have noted in our previous lessons, when the writer of Hebrews
wrote his letter, he was addressing Jewish believers that had grown weary
as they waited on God to come through on certain promises He had
made. In Hebrews 10:23, he said, "Let us hold fast the profession of our
faith without wavering; (for he is faithful that promised)."

We have seen that the words "hold fast" are a translation of the Greek word *katecho*, which is a compound of the words *kata* and *echo*. The word *kata* means *down*, and the word *echo* means *to hold, to possess,* or *to embrace.* It is a picture of wrapping one's arms around something tightly or putting all of one's weight on top of something so no one can take it away.

Holding fast the confession of our faith is very important because there are *dream thieves* all around us that will try to steal the dream or promise of God right out of our hands and out of our heart.

A Review of the Six Primary Dream Thieves

Dream Thief #1: *Time.* There is something about the passage of time that often fights against our faith and can cause us to question what we have heard from God. The enemy will use the passage of time to speak to you and try and get you to give up on God's promise. But even though things may appear to be put on hold, you can know that whatever God has said to you will come to pass "in due time" (*see* 1 Peter 5:6).

Dream Thief #2: *Friends.* The people you do life with love you and are concerned about your well-being. When they see that you've been waiting for a long time for your dream to come to pass and nothing has happened, they may question you and say, "Do you really think what you are trusting God to do is going to happen? You could be wrong. Maybe you should just give it up and move on."

When you hear those kinds of doubts, you need to resist the temptation to quit and embrace God's promise more tightly. If you know that you have heard from Him, don't let the voice of your friends cause you to abandon ship.

Dream Thief #3: *Family.* Generally speaking, no one is closer to you and loves you more than family. They are genuinely concerned about you, and out of their concern, they might say things like, "Are you absolutely sure that God spoke to you? You have misunderstood Him in the past, and maybe you have misunderstood what He has said in this situation. It may be best not to get your hopes up and just go on with your life."

When this happens, you must take time to go back over what the Lord has spoken to your heart and put all your weight on what He has promised so that no one can talk you out of it.

Dream Thief #4: *The Devil.* In addition to time, friends, and family, the voice of the devil himself will challenge your stance, mocking you and ridiculing you for what you've been believing. "Nothing's happening," he'll sneer, "and nothing is going to happen. You are nothing but a self-exalted dreamer trying to elevate yourself above others. Give up your dreaming and get back to the real world!"

Friend, don't believe the devil's lies. The reason he is speaking to you is because he knows you are a threat to his kingdom. Hold fast to what God has spoken to you and stay in agreement with Him. He will bring to pass what He has promised.

Dream Thief #5: *Neutrality.* This one is stealthy and gradually sneaks up on you as you grow tired of waiting. In fact, you may get so tired that eventually you come to a place where you say, "I used to want to see this dream come to pass, but now I couldn't care less if it happens or not." Neutrality sets in as passion for what God promised fades. This is a big enemy.

If you are slipping into neutral concerning your God-given dream, it's time for you to dig in your heels, wrap your arms around what He has said, and ask the Holy Spirit to fan into flames the fire you once had for the calling on your life.

Dream Thief #6: *Isolation.* Doing life alone is living in isolation. This never was and never will be God's will for your life. Instead, you are to live in reciprocal relationships with other believers, which is what we have focused on in Lessons 3 and 4, so if you need a review of this important principle, please refer back to those lessons.

We Are Not To Forsake the Assembling of Ourselves

When God's people grow weary and get discouraged, they tend to pull away from attending church. Although you might think this is a new practice, this was occurring among First Century believers, which is why the writer of Hebrews said:

Not forsaking the assembling of ourselves together, as the manner of some is; but exhorting one another: and so much the more, as ye see the day approaching.
                                                            — Hebrews 10:25

We saw that the word "forsaking" is the Greek word *egkataleipo*, which is a triple compound of three words: *en*, *kata*, and *leipo*. The word *en* means *in*, the word *kata* means *down*, and the word *leipo* means *far behind* or *to have a deficit*. When these three words are compounded to form the word *egkataleipo*, it describes *a person who is in a state of feeling down and out and far behind others*.

Moreover, this word describes the emotions of a person who is discouraged, depressed, and feels like everyone else has *surpassed* him. He senses a great deficit in his life, and that lack is so strong he lives feeling down, out, and far behind everyone else. Sadly, he has chosen to accept and settle into this defeated emotional state.

The truth is many believers begin to forsake church attendance when they are dealing with this level of discouragement. Rather than surround themselves with other faith-filled believers, they allow feelings of depression and despair to keep them at home. They will even tell you, "The last place I feel like being is around Christians who are filled with faith, lifting their hands, and shouting, 'Hallelujah!'" But the truth is, being around sincere, loving believers is the best place for them to be.

Friend, if you are feeling down, out, and lagging far behind everyone, don't give into your feelings. Don't let forsaking the assembling of yourself together with other believers become your custom. Do the opposite! Get together with other like-minded believers and allow the Spirit of God in them to strengthen you.

Skipping Church Is a Habit for Some

Looking again at Hebrews 10:25, it says, "Not forsaking the assembling of ourselves together, as the manner of some is; but exhorting one another: and so much the more, as ye see the day approaching." According to this verse, forsaking the assembling with other believers has become "the manner of some."

The word "manner" here is the Greek word *ethos*, and it describes *a custom, a behavior*, or *a habit*. Thus, for some people, it has become their custom, their behavior, or their habit to avoid church and avoid fellowshipping with other believers — especially when they are discouraged and need it most.

Friend, don't let that be you. If you're feeling down and out and need encouragement but you don't know where to get it, reach out to us at RENNER Ministries. We want to pray for you and encourage you in your faith.

The Holy Spirit Is Our 'Comforter'

The Bible goes on to say that instead of forsaking church gatherings, we should be "…exhorting one another: and so much the more, as ye see the day approaching" (Hebrews 10:25). In Greek, the word "exhorting" is the remarkable term *parakaleo*. As we learned in our previous lessons, the word *para* describes *something or someone that is parallel, alongside,* or *very close.* The second part of the word, *kaleo*, means *to call, to speak,* or *to beckon.*

When you compound these two words to form *parakaleo*, it describes *one that is called alongside and is as close as one can get*, and that person's assignment is *to speak, to beseech, to encourage,* and *to exhort another.* The word "exhort" is usually the way the word *parakaleo* is translated in the *King James Version.*

Interestingly, *parakaleo* is also the root word for the word "Comforter," which is one of the main titles Jesus assigns to the Holy Spirit. Four times in John's gospel, the Holy Spirit is called the "Comforter," which in Greek is *Parakletos*, taken from the Greek word *parakaleo.*

The Holy Spirit is the One who is *para* — called alongside us. He is in us, He is with us, He is alongside us, and He is speaking to us all the time — encouraging us, counseling us, correcting us, directing us, and coaching us, assuring us that we're going to make it and that we can do whatever we need to do.

When We Exhort Others, We Act Like the Holy Spirit

So when we come alongside other believers and begin to call out to them, we are acting like the Holy Spirit, ministering to others in the same way He ministers to us.

Something else that is fascinating about this word *parakaleo* is that in ancient times, it was used militarily to describe a commanding officer who would come alongside his troops, and before they were dispatched to fight in battle, he would speak to them and ready them for the fight. Along with describing the glories of victory, this officer would also detail the atrocities of war.

He would stir the troops to action like a commander. He would exhort them, encourage them, and equip them with the knowledge they would need to succeed in battle. By the time he was done, none of his soldiers were neutral about what they were about to face.

Amazingly, the Holy Spirit moved on the writer of Hebrews to use this same word *parakaleo* in Hebrews 10:25 to describe how we are to function in relationship with one another. Like fellow soldiers in God's army, we are to come alongside of other believers that are in the battle, fighting for their faith. As they're standing and believing that what God has pledged to them is going to come to pass, we are to call out to them like a commanding officer and say:

> Now is the time to hold fast. Wrap your arms around the dream God has given you, and don't let anyone take it from you. The dream thieves have come to jerk God's promise right out of your hands, but don't listen to them. You've been faithfully fighting for a long time, and you are right on the brink of receiving what you've been believing. Don't give up now! Keep taking one small step after the next and stay in the battle because the reward for victory is tremendous.

As believers, we have the privilege of coming alongside and in a parallel position to those who are struggling and calling out to them with words of encouragement. And just like the Holy Spirit is a Comforter to us, we can be a comforter to them. We can also be like a commanding officer. This is what the Bible means in Hebrews 10:25 when it says we are to "exhort one another." Again, these actions are reciprocal — we are to speak to others, and they are to speak to us.

'Call to Remembrance'
What God Has Already Done

Moving on from there, just seven verses later, the writer of Hebrews continued his instructions to these faith-weary saints — and to us — boldly saying:

But call to remembrance the former days, in which, after ye were illuminated, ye endured a great fight of afflictions.
— Hebrews 10:32

Notice it doesn't just say, "Remember." It says, "call to remembrance." This is a translation of the Greek word *anamimnesko*. The word *ana* is a prefix, which means *to do it again* and carries the idea of *upward movement*. The word *mimnesko* is actually a form of the Greek word *mneia*, which is the word for *a statue, a monument,* or *a memorial.*

Think about the purpose of a statue, monument, or memorial: It reminds you of something every time you see it and walk past it. It brings to remembrance a person or a group of people and all the wonderful deeds they did. It can also remind you of an extraordinary event that changed the course of history. Whatever the case, a statue or a monument is set up so that you never forget something.

What's interesting is that the word *mneia* is also the Greek term for *a grave*. The implication here is that if we don't deliberately remember important things, they will become *buried* over time. Memories that should never be forgotten get covered and hidden by the clutter and busy-ness of life. As weeks, months, and years pass, we begin to forget things, which is why the Holy Spirit prompted the writer of Hebrews to say, "But call to remembrance the former days..." (Hebrews 10:32). In other words, erect a statue, a monument, or a memorial in your life so that you should never ever forget what God has done.

And because the prefix *ana* is on the front of this word, it means we are to *repeat the action.* It carries the idea of *upward movement*, which means rather than let important things be buried and forgotten, we need to pull them up out of the grave, dust them off, and put them on a pedestal as a memorial so we can see them and be reminded of what God has done.

Essentially, the writer of Hebrews was telling these discouraged believers, "Hey, you need to go back to earlier times and remember again some of the blessings you've forgotten. You've allowed things like time, your friends and family, the devil, neutrality, and isolation to discourage you so deeply that you are forgetting some very important things. You need to recollect them — go back, dig them up, brush them off, and make them into a monument." All this meaning is in the phrase "call to remembrance."

Give Special Attention to the Times You Were 'Illuminated'

The writer of Hebrews specifically said, "But call to remembrance the former days, in which, after ye were *illuminated*...." (Hebrews 10:32). The word "illuminated" in Greek is the word *photidzo*. It is where we get the word for a *photograph*, and it describes *a brilliant flash of light that leaves a permanent and lasting impression*.

Keep in mind, the Jewish believers being addressed in Hebrews were struggling because they had not received any answer to their prayers. They were feeling "forsaken," which is a sense of being down, out, and lagging far behind everyone else. They had a deficit in their faith and were giving in to the feelings of depression and defeat.

The writer of Hebrews said, "Don't feel forsaken! Instead, go back and recollect the memories of the amazing things God did. Dig them up and pull them out of the grave. Brush them off and make them into a monument you can always see. Specifically, remember when you were filled with the Holy Spirit and you were first *illuminated*. The Spirit of God spoke to you so powerfully and gave you a word that jumped off the pages of Scripture and came alive in your heart."

Friend, the Lord is telling you to do the same thing. Rather than let memories of what God did be buried, He wants you to "call to remembrance" the former things. You are to pull up out of the grave the good memories that seem dead and buried and place them on a pedestal so that you can see them and never forget them — especially the times you were "illuminated."

Again, the word "illuminated" is the Greek word *photidzo*, and it describes *a brilliant flash of light that leaves a permanent and lasting impression*. Rick shared an example of a *photidzo* moment, telling of the time when God first spoke to him and instructed him to move his family to the former Soviet Union. That moment was like a brilliant flash of light that made a permanent and lasting impression on his life — a memory that he'll never forget. It is something he should always have on a pedestal in his mind.

Another *photidzo* moment Rick shared was the time he first understood that physical healing is included in the atonement of Jesus Christ. The moment he learned that the stripes Jesus took on His back and body paid for our healing was like a brilliant flash of light that left a permanent and lasting impression on him. These are the kinds of things we are never to forget.

In our next lesson, we will continue our dissection of Hebrews 10:32 and learn what the writer meant when saying, "…After ye were illuminated, ye endured a great fight of afflictions."

STUDY QUESTIONS

Study to shew thyself approved unto God, a workman that needeth not to be ashamed, rightly dividing the word of truth.
— 2 Timothy 2:15

1. Being a part of a vibrant, local church is very important. It allows you to be fed spiritually, serve others with your gifts, and experience the joy and power of God's corporate anointing as you partner with fellow believers in the work of the Church.

    • Do you have a church that you call "home"? If so, what church is it?

    • What do you like and enjoy most about your church family?

    • Do you take time before and after gatherings to talk and connect with others? If not, why?

    • In what area of ministry are you privileged to serve? Where do you feel needed and fulfilled?

    • If you're attending a church but you're not being spiritually fed, consider praying and asking the Holy Spirit to help you find an alive and Bible-believing church where you can connect and grow spiritually — or ask Him to reveal ways to get more involved at your home church.

PRACTICAL APPLICATION

**But be ye doers of the word, and not hearers only,
deceiving your own selves.
— James 1:22**

1. The phrase "call to remembrance" in Hebrews 10:32 is very similar
    to the principle of Psalm 77:11-12. Recalling to memory the good
    God has done and symbolically building a memorial of His works are
    important to remaining in our place of faith. Take time to remem-
    ber and meditate on the blessings God has provided for you in the
    past, including times of His protection and His provision. Give Him
    thanks and praise for His mercy, love, and kindness. He is certainly
    deserving of it!

2. Can you think of a time (or two) in your life when the Holy Spirit
    "illuminated" you regarding a specific Bible truth? What did He cause
    to leap off the pages of Scripture? How have divine revelations like
    these permanently changed your life?

3. Rick shared the "*photidzo* moment" when God first spoke to him
    and told him to move his family to the former Soviet Union. That
    moment really defined his calling. Do you remember the first time
    God spoke to you about His dream of greatness in *your* life? If so,
    what is the dream He gave you? In what ways can you see that He's
    been preparing you for what's coming?

LESSON 6

TOPIC

Are You Standing Your Ground?

SCRIPTURES

1. **Hebrews 10:32** — But call to remembrance the former days, in
    which, after ye were illuminated, ye endured a great fight of afflictions.

2. **John 15:7** — If ye abide in me, and my words abide in you, ye shall
    ask what ye will, and it shall be done unto you.

3. **Hebrews 10:33** — Partly, whilst ye were made a gazingstock both by reproaches and afflictions; and partly, whilst ye became companions of them that were so used.

GREEK WORDS

1. "call to remembrance" — ἀναμιμνήσκω (*anamimnesko*): made up of the prefix ἀνα (*ana*), which means to do it again and carries the idea of upward movement, and the word μνεία (*mneia*), which is the word for a statue, monument, or memorial; the word μνεία (*mneia*) is also the word for a grave

2. "illuminated" — φωτίζω (*photidzo*): where we get the English word for photograph; a brilliant flash of light that leaves a permanent and lasting impression

3. "fight" — ἄθλησις (*athlesis*): the word from which the English word athlete is derived; contest, struggle, conflict; a struggle, as in an athletic contest

4. "afflictions" — πάθημα (*pathema*): mental or emotional suffering

5. "endured" — ὑπομένω (*hupomeno*): a compound word made up of the words ὑπο (*hupo*), which depicts being under something, and μένω (*meno*), which means to stay or to abide; the resulting compound word depicts a person who is under a very heavy load, but he has made a decision that despite the weight and pressure, he will not move; one man translated ὑπομένω (*hupomeno*) as hang-in-there power; another man translated it as staying power; ὑπομένω (*hupomeno*) also depicts soldiers who have been commanded to maintain the territory they have gained, regardless of any resistance; the Early Church called ὑπομένω (*hupomeno*) the queen of all virtues

6. "early days" — πρότερον (*proteron*): previously, before, formerly

7. "gazingstock" — θεατρίζω (*theatridzo*): derived from θέατρον (*theatron*), meaning a theater or a place for public show

SYNOPSIS

Once you finally begin to understand the Word of God and have a grasp on what He wants to do in and through your life, the devil and his demonic forces will step up their game, increasing their attacks in an all-out attempt to get you out of your place of faith. The enemy knows that if you stay where you're supposed to be and remain in faith, God is going to move on your behalf, and you will receive what you're believing for.

So if you are feeling assaulted by overwhelming circumstances and difficult people, don't give up! Press into Jesus and stand your ground. More than likely, you're right on the brink of the breakthrough you've been waiting for, and as Scripture says, "…At just the right time we will reap a harvest of blessing if we don't give up" (Galatians 6:9 *NLT*).

The emphasis of this lesson:

When you receive a word from God and are illuminated, it is often followed by "a great fight of afflictions." The enemy will assault your mind and emotions in an attempt to get you to abandon your place of faith. But if you'll make a decision to stand your ground — *despite the pressure or resistance coming against you* **— you will receive what God has promised.**

'Call to Remembrance' the Good Things God Has Done

In previous lessons, we noted that the writer of Hebrews was speaking to a group of Jewish believers who were really struggling in their faith. They had been waiting and waiting for the manifestation of God's promises to become a reality in their lives. But when it seemed that there was no breakthrough in sight, they began to believe they had misunderstood what God had said and were tempted to let go of His promises and move on with their lives. That's when the writer of Hebrews said:

> **But call to remembrance the former days, in which, after ye were illuminated, ye endured a great fight of afflictions.**
> **— Hebrews 10:32**

We've seen that the phrase "call to remembrance" is a translation of the Greek word *anamimnesko*. It is a compound of the words *ana* and *mneia*. The word *ana* means *to do it again* and carries the idea of *upward movement*, and the word *mneia* is the word for *a statue, a monument*, or *a memorial*. It is also the word for *a grave* or *a tomb*.

When you consider the meaning of this Greek compound word *anamimnesko*, which is translated "call to remembrance" in Hebrews 10:32, you find that the writer of Hebrews was saying there are some memories that should never be entombed. The memories of what God did for you in the early years of your walk with Him should never be buried or forgotten. Especially the times when you were enlightened to wonderful truths that changed your life.

Very often, through the busyness and troubles of life, it seems those priceless early memories become covered up and buried with the "clutter" of life. The phrase "call to remembrance" emphatically urges us to purposely and repeatedly pull up (*ana*) those memories out of the grave and turn them into a statue or a monument (*mneia*).

Again, the purpose of a statue, monument, or memorial is to remind us of something every time we see it or walk past it. It brings to remembrance the wonderful deeds done by a person or a group of people. The use of this word *anamimnesko* is God's way of telling us, "Get those precious memories of what I first did in your life up and out of the grave! Dust off the dirt and make them into *a memorial, a monument*, or *a statue* that you keep on a "pedestal" and constantly in full view in your life."

Rick shared the precious memory of when he was first illuminated about the baptism in the Holy Spirit. It was a thrilling time, and ever since then he has been walking in the power of the Spirit for many years. Likewise, the time when God first called Rick and his family to move to the former Soviet Union more than three decades ago is also a special memory of his. These things could easily be buried by the busyness of life, but because they're so foundational to his faith, he has learned to put them on a pedestal and never forget them.

In the same way, if God spoke something to you, but it has been a while since then and it hasn't come to pass yet, don't let the clutter of life bury what He has spoken. Pull it out of the grave, dust it off, and put it back on a pedestal so that you're always confronted with what He said to you. Never forget it. Let it be like a monument, a statue, or a memorial in your life.

Moments of 'Illumination' Are Powerful and Priceless

Hebrews 10:32 goes on to say, "But call to remembrance the former days, in which, after ye were illuminated…." The words "former days" in Greek are translated from the Greek word *proteron*, which means the *early days*. It is pointing to a past experience when you were *illuminated*. In Greek, the word for "illuminated" is *photidzo*, and we learned in our previous lesson that it describes *a brilliant flash of light that leaves a permanent and lasting impression*. It is from where we get the English word for *photograph*.

If you are old enough, you may remember that cameras used to have big flashbulbs attached to them, and every time you took a picture, that bulb would flash a brilliant burst of light, enabling the film in the camera to capture the memorable image — an image that was permanent and lasting.

Similarly, there are times in our lives when God supernaturally opens the eyes of our understanding with the brilliant light of His truth. Suddenly, we are illuminated with a revelation we have never seen before. For example, maybe you were illuminated about the healing that comes through the stripes Jesus received (*see* 1 Peter 2:24), or maybe you received a revelation that it is God's will for you to prosper to the same degree that your soul prospers (*see* 3 John 2).

Every time we experience one of these "wake-up moments," we see something for the first time that we've never seen before. These moments of illumination (*photidzo*) are like a giant flash of light that leaves a permanent, lasting impression on our lives. These memories from our "former days" (*proteron*) are what the writer of Hebrews told us to dig up, pull out of the grave, and place on a pedestal. They are to become a monument, a statue, or a memorial that we never forget.

A 'Fight of Afflictions' Usually Follows Illumination

It is also important to realize that after those times of illumination, we can expect some resistance. Hebrews 10:32 says, "…After ye were illuminated, ye endured a great fight of afflictions." Here we see that a great fight of affliction usually follows illumination, and there are examples of this all throughout the Bible. In fact, in Hebrews 11, the very next chapter, the writer lists a series of people who experienced a great fight of affliction just after they received an illuminating word from the Lord.

Enoch received a word from God that he would never die. Noah was illuminated by God and was told to build an ark, and that through that ark, God would save his family and, ultimately, the entire human race. God also illuminated Abraham with a divine call to leave his country, his family, and all he had known. Sarah, Abraham's wife, was also illuminated with the divine promise that she would give birth to a baby even in her old age. Then there was Isaac, Jacob, Joseph, and on and on the list goes — each person being illuminated with a word from God that left a permanent and lasting impression on their lives.

But after receiving their God-given revelations, each of these individuals was faced with "a great fight of afflictions" to overcome in order to step into the manifestation of what God had promised. In the original text, the word "fight" is the Greek word *athlesis*, which is the word from which the English word *athlete* is derived. It describes a *contest, a struggle*, or *a conflict*; a *struggle*, as in *an athletic contest*. Just like athletes struggle and fight other athletes, when we've received a word from God, we are thrown into a real fight with the enemy. Furthermore, the writer of Hebrews says it is a fight of "afflictions." This word is a form of the Greek word *pathema*, which describes *mental or emotional suffering*

Here we find that one of the greatest fights you will ever face is when the devil attacks you in your mind and emotions. When your mind is suffering, that is when you're most tempted to give up. The enemy will come against you with thoughts like, *Why are you wasting your time? You've been waiting and waiting for something that's never going to happen. If you had really heard from God, it would have happened by now. It's time to cut your losses and move on.* Satan's aim is to coax you out of your place of faith by any means possible.

'Endurance' Is the Power To Stay Put

When you find yourself embroiled in a *fight of afflictions*, you need the grace of God to endure. That is what these new Jewish believers did — they had *endured* the mental attacks. This word "endured" in Hebrews 10:32 is the remarkable Greek word *hupomeno*, a compound of the words *hupo*, which depicts *being under something*, and *meno*, which means *to stay* or *to abide*.

The word *meno* is also found in John 15:7, where Jesus said, "If ye abide in me, and my words abide in you, ye shall ask what ye will, and it shall be done unto you." The word "abide" in this verse is the Greek word *meno*, which means *to stay* or *to abide*. Thus, we could translate Jesus' words, "If you abide in Me — if you're fixed and unmoving in Me, and My words are fixed and unmoving in you — you will ask what you will, and it will be done unto you."

When the words *hupo* and *meno* are compounded to form *hupomeno*, it depicts *a person who is under a very heavy load, but he has made a decision that despite the weight and pressure, he will not move*. This individual has taken on the attitude of someone who says, "I don't care how heavy the load is or how long it takes. It doesn't matter how much pressure comes against me to move me out of my place of faith. I have made a decision that, even if the load I'm under gets enormously heavy (*hupo*), I choose to stay in my place. I know what God said and what He illuminated in my heart, and I'm not budging, flinching, or moving. If anyone is going to move, it's not going to be me. I'm going to stay put and hold tightly to the promise God gave me."

One man translated the word *hupomeno* as *hang-in-there power*. Another man translated it as *staying power*. Interestingly, the word *hupomeno* also depicts soldiers who have been commanded to maintain the territory they have gained, regardless of any resistance they have to confront. The Early Church called *hupomeno* — translated here as "endured" — the queen of all virtues. They understood that by having *hupomeno* — the supernatural power to stay put, hang in there, and not give up — the question is not *if* you're going to receive an answer to your prayers, but *when* you're going to receive.

Our Decision To Trust God Puts Us Centerstage

In the very next verse, the writer of Hebrews continued by saying, "Partly, whilst ye were made a gazingstock both by reproaches and afflictions; and partly, whilst ye became companions of them that were so used" (Hebrews 10:33).

What does it mean to be a *gazingstock*? As you may have correctly guessed, part of the meaning involves someone gazing at you, but that is not all. This word "gazingstock" is a translation of the Greek word *theatridzo*, which is where we get the English word for *a theater*, and its use here indicates that when you make a bold declaration of faith, suddenly you leave private life and find yourself standing on the world's stage with everyone watching you.

When people hear your bold declaration, it is as if they buy a ticket to the show to see if what you have declared is really going to take place. Indeed, when you make a declaration of faith, people will begin watching your life.

Friend, if you know that God spoke to you, hold fast to what He said and stay in your place of faith until you receive the manifestation of what you know He promised. Call to remembrance all the ways He has come through for you in the past — especially when He first illuminated you with truths that transformed your life. God was faithful before, and He will be faithful again!

STUDY QUESTIONS

Study to shew thyself approved unto God, a workman that needeth not to be ashamed, rightly dividing the word of truth.
— 2 Timothy 2:15

1. When you think of the people in the Bible who received a word or promise from the Lord and then experienced a great fight of affliction, who comes to mind? What is it about that person's story that is most impactful or encouraging?

2. In order to endure and experience victory in the fight of our afflictions, we need a moment-by-moment supply of the Holy Spirit's power flowing in our life. Take time to meditate on these promises from God's Word, guaranteeing the Spirit's power in your life.

   You have armed me with strength for the battle; you have subdued my enemies under my feet.
   — 2 Samuel 22:40 (*NLT*)

   He [God] gives power to the faint and weary, and to him who has no might He increases strength [causing it to multiply and making it to abound]. Even youths shall faint and be weary, and [selected] young men shall feebly stumble and fall exhausted; But those who wait for the Lord [who expect, look for, and hope in Him] shall change and renew their strength and power; they shall lift their wings and mount up [close to God] as eagles [mount up to the sun]; they shall run and not be weary, they shall walk and not faint or become tired.
   — Isaiah 40:29-31 (*AMPC*)

   But He gives us more and more grace (power of the Holy Spirit, to meet this evil tendency and all others fully). That is why He says, God sets Himself against the proud and haughty, but gives

grace [continually] to the lowly (those who are humble enough to receive it).

—James 4:6 (*AMPC*)

PRACTICAL APPLICATION

But be ye doers of the word, and not hearers only,
deceiving your own selves.
—James 1:22

1. What "great fight of afflictions" have you had to walk through in the past in order to step into the manifestation of what God promised? How did God guide you, provide for you, and protect you through all the circumstances? How does remembering these details give you hope that you will emerge victoriously out of your current challenges?

2. Would you like to receive more illumination of truth from the Holy Spirit? God wants to give it to you! Take this prayer that Paul prayed in Ephesians 1:17-19 (*AMPC*) and make it your own:

   ...Father, grant me a spirit of wisdom and revelation [of insight into mysteries and secrets] in the [deep and intimate] knowledge of You, by having the eyes of my heart flooded with light, so that I can know and understand the hope to which You have called me, and how rich is Your glorious inheritance in the saints (Your set-apart ones). Enable me [so that I can know and understand] what is the immeasurable and unlimited and surpassing greatness of Your power in and for us who believe, as demonstrated in the working of Your mighty strength. In Jesus' name. Amen!

LESSON 7

TOPIC

Will You Shine Under Scrutiny?

SCRIPTURES

1. **Hebrews 10:32-33** — But call to remembrance the former days, in which, after ye were illuminated, ye endured a great fight of afflictions; partly, whilst ye were made a gazingstock both by reproaches and afflictions....

2. **Hebrews 10:34** — For ye had compassion of me in my bonds, and took joyfully the spoiling of your goods, knowing in yourselves that ye have in heaven a better and an enduring substance.

3. **Hebrews 10:35** — Cast not away therefore your confidence, which hath great recompence of reward.

GREEK WORDS

1. "illuminated" — **φωτίζω** (*photidzo*): where we get the English word for photograph; a brilliant flash of light that leaves a permanent and lasting impression

2. "gazingstock" — **θεατρίζω** (*theatridzo*): derived from **θέατρον** (*theatron*), meaning a theater or a place for public show

3. "reproaches" — **ὀνειδισμός** (*oneidismos*): insults and insulting behavior from people

4. "afflictions" — **θλῖψις** (*thlipsis*): heavy duty, high-pressured life situations that can break a person

5. "spoiling" — **ἁρπαγή** (*harpage*): plunder or robbery

6. "cast not away" — **ἀποβάλλω** (*apoballo*): **ἀπο** (*apo*), which means away, and the word **βάλλω** (*ballo*), meaning to throw; as a compound, **ἀποβάλλω** (*apoballo*) is to throw off or to cast away

7. "confidence" — **παρρησία** (*parresia*): a bold, frank, forthright kind of speech; a declaration

SYNOPSIS

Did you know that people are watching you? At home, at work, at church, and in the community, the eyes of others — Christian and non-Christian alike — are looking at how you live and how you respond to difficult situations. The question is, what are they seeing?

Second Corinthians 5:20 (*NLT*) says, "…We are Christ's ambassadors; God is making his appeal through us. We speak for Christ…." Clearly, God wants our lives to speak an appealing message of who He is, and as we trust Him to fulfill His promises, He wants our lives to be a spectacle of enduring faith all the way to victory.

The emphasis of this lesson:

Once we are illuminated with a word from God, we symbolically leave the private sector and take "centerstage" for all to see. We become a spectacle and can suffer insulting behavior and high-pressure situations that try to break us. But if we will not cast away our confidence and hold fast to our confession of faith, we will reap the reward we seek.

A Quick Review of Hebrews 10:32

To encourage the new Jewish believers who were weary from waiting for the manifestation of God's promises, the writer of Hebrews urged them by saying, "…Call to remembrance the former days in which, after ye were illuminated, ye endured a great fight of afflictions" (Hebrews 10:32). Before diving into verse 33, here is a quick review of what we've learned from verse 32:

The word "illuminated" is the Greek word *photidzo*.

It is the term from which the English word *photograph* is derived, and it describes *a brilliant flash of light that leaves a permanent and lasting impression*. In Hebrews 10:32, the writer was reminding his readers to dig up and dust off the precious memories of what God had done in the past and put them on a "pedestal" to never be forgotten.

Most importantly, these believers were to remember the "former," or *early*, days when they were first illuminated with truth that exploded on the screen of their hearts, leaving a permanent and lasting impression on their lives.

"A great fight of afflictions" seems to follow moments of great revelation (Hebrews 10:32). "Afflictions" are bouts of *mental and emotional suffering* that are common to all believers in all generations. In other words, it is normal for the devil to come after you when you're illuminated.

Martin Luther is a wonderful example. When he was illuminated with the truth — that salvation was by faith and not works — the world was living in the Dark Ages. Shortly after receiving the revelation that "the just shall live by faith," the devil went into overdrive to try and push Luther out of his place of faith. In fact, Satan was so terrified of this one man that he did everything he could to stop him. But Martin Luther did not yield or surrender. Instead, he endured (*hupomeno*) and stayed in his place of faith.

Remarkably, this one illuminated man with one word from God helped usher the world out of the Dark Ages, which demonstrates the power of even one person who is illuminated.

What has God said to you? In what ways has He *illuminated* your life? What revelations of truth have made a permanent and lasting impression on you?

For Rick and his family, one of the most important illuminations they received was when God called them to the former Soviet Union. It was like a brilliant flash of light that showed them where they were to move and what they were to begin doing. Still, when Rick was first illuminated with his calling, the devil didn't just sit on the sidelines and watch Rick do God's work. On the contrary, the devil opposed and attacked him, and he has continued to do so in multiple ways because he's terrified of anyone that is illuminated.

Illuminated people change history. When you are illuminated by the Spirit of God, you can change your family, your city, your church, and your life. All it takes is one word from God that you decide to hold on to until it manifests and becomes reality.

What Does It Mean To Be a 'Gazingstock'?

The writer of Hebrews went on to describe the afflictions we face, saying, "Partly, whilst ye were made a gazingstock both by reproaches and afflictions" (Hebrews 10:33). We touched on this passage at the end of Lesson 6, but let's review what we learned and go a bit deeper into its meaning.

In Greek, the word for "gazingstock" is *theatridzo*, which is derived from the word *theatron*, meaning *a theater* or *a place for public show*. The use of this word here tells us that when we are illuminated and receive a word from God, we symbolically leave the private sector and take our place on "centerstage" for all to see. Suddenly, it is as if people begin to buy tickets to sit and watch what we're going to do.

Onlookers will say things like, "Is he really going to do what he said he's going to do?" and "She said that promise was from God, but is it *really* going to come to pass?"

Like it or not, anytime you make a declaration of faith, people begin to develop opinions. They talk quietly among themselves, saying things like, "What do you think? Did he really hear from God, or is he just imagining things? And if he heard from God, do you think he has the stamina to see his dream become a reality?"

If you think about it, people who don't have a word from God are virtually invisible. No one talks about them, and no one watches them. The fact that you are a "gazingstock" means people are watching the show of your life. They want to see you in act one, act two, act three, and act four. They're watching to see if you're going to make it to the end and experience the victory you've proclaimed, or if you're going to forget your lines and stumble off the stage.

Since people are "buying theater tickets" to watch your life and find out if what you said God has promised is going to come to pass, make sure you give them the best performance they've ever seen! Show them how faith works and let them see what it means to operate in endurance (*hupomeno*). That is, give them a demonstration of how to stick it out, stay put, never give up, and outlast the enemy. Let them watch you push through every obstacle and overcome every hindrance as you make your way to victory at the end of the show.

When others watch you successfully walk in faith — not surrendering, not budging, and not flinching when trouble comes — it will encourage them to get out of their seats and get on the stage themselves. God has a specific part for them to play in His plans, and by seeing someone else walk in faith and do well, they will have hope and be encouraged to do something by faith too.

God's People Have Always Been a 'Gazingstock'

In the late 1970s, Oral Roberts began proclaiming that God had told him to build the City of Faith, which was a massive complex in Tulsa, Oklahoma. Of course, people began ridiculing him and laughing at him, and several in the newspapers and media began denigrating him publicly.

Clearly, Oral became a "gazingstock" just as the Bible says in Hebrews 10:33. People bought tickets to the show and began watching his life. Yet, despite all the critics, Oral continued in faith and did succeed in completing the building complex in 1981. By that point, there was nothing more for critics to laugh about because he did what he said.

Noah is another example of a "gazingstock." God told him to build an ark because a worldwide flood was coming that would destroy all life on the earth. In obedience, Noah began building the ark when he was 500 years old, and he worked on it for about 100 years. Can you imagine the jokes at Noah's expense that were circulating throughout society? Noah's critics likely snickered and said things like, "A flood? What's a flood? This old man is crazy!"

At that point in human history, no one had seen a flood. In fact, no one had even experienced rainfall. All the earth's vegetation was watered by a mist that came up from the ground (*see* Genesis 2:5-6). Amazingly, regardless of the ridicule brought against Noah and his family, they kept laboring on the massive ship that God had commissioned him to build.

Every time the cynics drew near to make fun and laugh at Noah, he just ignored them and kept working. Public opinion did not matter or sway him one bit because he had been illuminated with a word from God. Thankfully, he held fast to the confession of his faith and didn't let go of the illumination he had received (*see* Hebrews 10:23). At the age of 600, Noah finished the ark and entered it with his family (*see* Genesis 7:5-7). And because he stayed in his place of faith, we are here today!

As Believers, We Will Experience 'Reproach' and 'Afflictions'

Looking once more at Hebrews 10:33, we read, "Partly, whilst ye were made a gazingstock both by reproaches and afflictions...." The fact that the Bible mentions both *reproaches* and *afflictions* means these are two different things. In Greek, the word "reproaches" is *oneidismos*, and it describes *insults and insulting behavior from people.* As many sit and watch, we can expect that some will insult us with derogatory language and hurtful behavior (*oneidismos*).

In addition to "reproaches," we are also subjected to "afflictions" (*see* Hebrews 10:33). This word is a translation of the Greek word *thlipsis*, describing *heavy duty, high-pressured life situations that can break a person.* This may include a lack of money to fulfill your dream, an attack of sickness on your body, or a slammed door that was once open. These are all examples of the "afflictions" that Satan can bring against you to pressure you to move out of your place of faith.

When reproaches and afflictions come, remember that the attacks are not about you. They are about the word of illumination you received. The devil hates the fact that God gave you a promise, a pledge, or an assignment. He knows that if you stay in your place of faith and do what God said, lives are going to be changed for the better. Therefore, he stirs up storms all around you in an attempt to get you to abandon your assignment. He sends people to discourage you with dismal, insulting, denigrating words, trying to get you to quit.

If insulting behavior doesn't work, he'll send *heavy duty, high-pressured life situations* against you (*thlipsis*) to try to crush you and totally break you, which is why this teaching is so important. If you are aware of Satan's tactics, you can prepare for them and work with the Holy Spirit to develop the endurance (*hupomeno*) you need in order to stay in your place of faith.

Illuminated People Are Impossible To Keep Down

After the writer of Hebrews informed us of the reproaches and afflictions we will face, he shifted his focus to talk about the kindness of his readers who came to his aid when he was in need. In Hebrews 10:34, he wrote, "For ye had compassion of me in my bonds, and took joyfully the spoiling of your goods knowing in yourselves that ye have in heaven a better and an enduring substance."

The word "spoiling" is in this passage is the Greek word *harpage*, which means *plunder* or *robbery*. When the writer of Hebrews was in chains, these new Jewish believers had compassion on him, even when faced with being robbed of their goods, which many First Century believers experienced. They were often ridiculed and treated badly by both pagans and Jews alike.

These believers suffered joyfully, knowing in themselves that they had something way better waiting for them in Heaven (*see* Hebrews 10:34). How did they know this truth "in themselves"? They knew because they had been illuminated by God, and people who are illuminated are impossible to keep down! It didn't matter how much of their earthly goods were stolen. They had been illuminated, and they knew that even if they lost everything, they still had a reward in Heaven that could not be stolen — eternal life.

'Cast Not Away' Your Confidence

In light of this great confidence these new believers possessed, the writer of Hebrews went on to urge them, "Cast not away therefore your confidence, which hath great recompence of reward" (Hebrews 10:35).

Notice the opening phrase "cast not away." It is a translation of the remarkable Greek word *apoballo*, a compound of the words *apo* and *ballo*. The word *apo* means *away*, and the word *ballo* means *to throw*. As a compound, the word *apoballo* means *to throw off, to cast away, to discard*, or *to get rid of*.

Hence, the writer of Hebrews was telling his readers, both then and now, "Don't throw off, discard, or get rid of your confidence, because it has great recompense of reward." The word "confidence" here is the Greek word *parresia*, which describes *a bold, frank, forthright kind of speech* or *a declaration*. In the context of Hebrews 10:35, it was their *bold declaration of faith*.

Remember, the people being addressed in Hebrews were new Jewish believers who had been waiting and waiting for what God had promised to come to pass. And now the *dream thieves* were speaking to them, trying to get them to move out of their place of faith.

> *Time* was saying, "Surely, if this were going to happen, it would've happened by now."

> *Friends* were saying, "Are you sure you've heard from God? Maybe you misunderstood."

> *Family*, who really loved them were saying, "Hasn't your life been on pause long enough? Why don't you just forget all these things and move on?"

> *Satan* mocked them, saying, "Who do you think you are? You're nothing but a derelict dreamer."

> *Neutrality* had also set in due to the extremely long wait, causing them to become so tired that they no longer cared if what they had been believing for ever came to pass.

It is at this point that *isolation*, dream thief number six, typically shows up. And when a person is in isolation, it's much easier for him to surrender to exhaustion and give up.

With all these voices speaking — just like they occasionally speak to you — these believers were tempted to cast away their confidence. They were on the verge of saying, "I wish I had never received this promise from God. Then I could have gone on with my life. Instead, I've been stuck in this same place year after year, waiting for this dream to happen. Meanwhile, all my friends have gone on with their lives, and I just keep waiting for this thing God promised."

Sound familiar? Everyone experiences frustrating times like these at one point or another. You may be going through one right now. The good news is, if the mental and emotional assault is the hardest and heaviest it has ever been, more than likely you are on the brink of your breakthrough!

Friend, now is not the time to throw in the towel and throw away what you believe God spoke to you. Now is the time to get a tighter grip on your confession of faith and ask God for a greater level of His grace to stay in your place of faith. "Cast not away therefore your confidence, which hath great recompence of reward" (Hebrews 10:35). We will learn more about the meaning of this verse in our next lesson.

STUDY QUESTIONS

**Study to shew thyself approved unto God, a workman that
needeth not to be ashamed, rightly dividing the word of truth.
— 2 Timothy 2:15**

1. What do First Corinthians 10:13, First Peter 5:8-10, and Romans 8:17 and 18 tell us about the troubles and afflictions we as Christians face?
2. According to Jesus' words in Matthew 5:10-12, what blessings or rewards come as a result of suffering "reproaches" and "afflictions"? Also consider Paul's words in Second Corinthians 4:16-18 as you answer.

PRACTICAL APPLICATION

**But be ye doers of the word, and not hearers only,
deceiving your own selves.
— James 1:22**

1. Anytime you make a declaration of faith, people begin watching your life and developing opinions about you. Can you think of someone

who was watching you, but you didn't learn about it until much later? Who was it, and what kind of effect did your life have on that person? Whose life are you watching? What attitudes and actions has that person demonstrated that have encouraged you in your faith and been an example for you to follow?

2. Proverbs 10:17 (*AMPC*) says, "He who heeds instruction and correction is [not only himself] in the way of life [but also] *is a way of life for others....*" Overall, how would you say your life is impacting others — especially those closest to you? Would they describe you as a mostly positive, a neutral, or a negative influence? What adjustments do you sense the Holy Spirit is asking you to make so you can put on a better "show" for God's glory?

LESSON 8

TOPIC

Are You Bold Enough To Wait?

SCRIPTURES

1. **Proverbs 13:12** — Hope deferred maketh the heart sick....

2. **Hebrews 10:35** — Cast not away therefore your confidence, which hath great recompence of reward.

3. **Mark 10:50** — And he, casting away his garment, rose, and came to Jesus.

4. **Hebrews 10:23** — Let us hold fast the profession of our faith without wavering; (for he is faithful that promised).

5. **Hebrews 10:36-37** — For ye have need of patience, that, after ye have done the will of God, ye might receive the promise. For yet a little while, and he that shall come will come, and will not tarry.

6. **Hebrews 10:38-39** — Now the just shall live by faith: But if any man draw back, my soul shall have no pleasure in him. But we are not of them who draw back unto perdition; but of them that believe to the saving of the soul.

GREEK WORDS

1. "cast not away" — **ἀποβάλλω** (*apoballo*): **ἀπο** (*apo*), which means away, and the word **βάλλω** (*ballo*), meaning to throw; as a compound, **ἀποβάλλω** (*apoballo*) is to throw off or to cast away

2. "confidence" — **παρρησία** (*parresia*): a bold, frank, forthright kind of speech; a declaration

3. "great recompence of reward" — **μισθαποδοσία** (*misthapodosia*): a compound of the words **μισθα** (*mistha*), meaning payment, salary, or reward; and **ποδοσία** (*podosia*) that comes from the word **ποδοσ** (*podos*), which is the word for feet

4. "need" — **χρεία** (*chreian*): a deficit, necessity, lack, requirement

5. "patience" — **ὑπομένω** (*hupomeno*): a compound word made up of the words **ὑπο** (*hupo*), which depicts being under something, and **μένω** (*meno*), which means to stay or to abide; the resulting compound word depicts a person who is under a very heavy load, but he has made a decision that despite the weight and pressure, he will not move; one man translated **ὑπομένω** (*hupomeno*) as hang-in-there power; another man translated it as staying power; **ὑπομένω** (*hupomeno*) also depicts soldiers who have been commanded to maintain the territory they have gained, regardless of any resistance; the Early Church called **ὑπομένω** (*hupomeno*) the queen of all virtues

6. "receive" — **κομίζω** (*komidzo*): to be paid

7. "he" — **ὁ** (*ho*): the thing

8. "little" — **μικρὸν** (*mikron*): the word from which the English word microscope is derived; small, little, least

9. "tarry" — **χρονίζω** (*chronidzo*): to be late; to be delayed

SYNOPSIS

If God has given you a promise or illuminated your life with a special revelation, the enemy will fight hard to get you to give up on what God has said. Nevertheless, if you will draw strength from the Greater One living in you — the Spirit of God — and if you'll be determined to do God's will without surrendering to the pressure brought on by the *dream thieves*, you will see His power bring about what you've been believing will come to pass.

The emphasis of this lesson:

The thing you've been waiting for is right in front of you. In fact, it's on its feet moving in your direction. As you choose to stay in your place of faith and cooperate with the Holy Spirit, He will develop in you the patience you need to inherit and flourish in the promise of God. So don't cast away your bold declaration of faith.

Recognize and Guard Against the Six Dream Thieves

As we have noted throughout this series, the book of Hebrews is written to believers who were very discouraged. They had been dealing with the same *dream thieves* that all of us face at various times in our lives.

Dream Thief #1: *Time*. Time has a way of speaking to you. Proverbs 13:12 says, "Hope deferred maketh the heart sick...." When what you've been hoping for hasn't manifested for a long, long time, the delay has a way of wearing you down to the point that you just want to walk away and forget what God has said. Indeed, time has a voice, and you must resist it.

Dream Thief #2: *Friends*. Your friends really care about you, and out of their love and deep concern they may try to talk you out of continuing to wait for what God has promised.

Dream Thief #3: *Family*. Family can be one of the strongest voices in your life. It is often the case that one loves you more than they do, and if they see that you've been stuck in the same place, believing for something that still hasn't come to pass, they may become so brokenhearted that they try to coax you out of your place of faith.

Dream Thief #4: *The devil*. You must learn to recognize and resist the voice of the devil. He will mock you, condemn you, and accuse you whenever he can, telling you things like, "You are so stupid to keep waiting on God's 'promise.' It's never going to happen. You are damaged goods and don't deserve to be used by Him." Remember, the devil is a liar and the father of lies (*see* John 8:44). Don't listen to him.

Dream Thief #5: *Neutrality.* This is the voice you begin to hear when you become exhausted from the wait. Neutrality says, "I'm so tired of this and worn out from waiting, I really don't care if it happens or not." Whatever you do, don't give in to this voice. Keep believing and don't let go of God's promise.

Dream Thief #6: *Isolation.* Isolation and its negative effects are exponential. Living in a place of isolation is serious, because it causes you to become more vulnerable and victimized by the other five dream thieves.

If you feel like you're living in isolation, you need to get into a church or home group where you can have reciprocal friendships. This is where people speak into your life, and you speak into theirs. If you don't have a place like that, let the *Renner Ministries* team be your place. Call us or send us an email so that we can pray for you and encourage you to stay in your place of faith.

A New Testament Example
of What It Means To 'Cast Away'

To the weary Hebrew believers who were about to give up on God's promises, the writer of Hebrews said, "Cast not away therefore your confidence, which hath great recompence of reward" (Hebrews 10:35). As we saw in Lesson 7, this verse is simply *packed* with meaning.

First, notice again the phrase "cast not away." This is a translation of the Greek word *apoballo*, which is a compound of the words *apo*, meaning *away*, and the word *ballo*, meaning *to throw*. When these two words are compounded to form *apoballo*, the new word means *to throw off* or *to cast away*. It carries the idea of throwing something so far away that you can no longer reach over and pick it up and retrieve it because you've put so much space between you and that object.

A great example of this word in the New Testament is found in Mark's gospel in the story of a blind man named Bartimaeus, who really wanted to move from where he was and get to Jesus. The Bible says that while he was sitting on the side of the road, he heard that Jesus was passing by. Bartimaeus called out to Jesus, and the Lord invited him to come to Him. But there was something hindering Bartimaeus from getting up and getting to Jesus. Mark 10:50 says, "And he [Bartimaeus], *casting away* his garment, rose, and came to Jesus."

In this verse, the words "casting away" are translated from *apoballo*, the same Greek word translated as "cast not away" in Hebrews 10:35. Bartimaeus was tired of being where he was and desperately wanted to get to Jesus, but his garment was wrapped around him and was a hindrance. So to get to Jesus, he cast it away (*apoballo*). He literally grabbed hold of his garment and said, 'This thing is not going to bind me or keep me sitting here any longer," and he threw it so far away from himself that he couldn't reach over to pick it up again.

'Confidence' Is a Bold Declaration of Faith

Hebrews 10:35 continues, "Cast not away therefore your confidence...." The word "confidence" here is the Greek word *parresia*, which describes *confidence* or *a bold, frank, forthright kind of speech*. In context here, it is *a bold declaration of faith*.

Indeed, faith has a voice! Real faith speaks, and its voice is bold, not puny.

Real faith says…

- "God is going to do what He said!" (*see* Numbers 23:19).
- "I am healed by the stripes of Jesus!" (*see* 1 Peter 2:24).
- "I planted good seed, and I have a good harvest coming my direction!" (*see* Galatians 6:7).

Again, the voice of faith is not weak or mousey. Real faith is bold, candid, forthright, and confident — that's how faith speaks. These believers the writer of Hebrews was addressing had initially been voicing their faith with great confidence. We know this because Hebrews 10:35 instructed them not to *give up* voicing their faith, indicating that they had already been making a bold declaration of faith. For quite some time, they had been confidently declaring what God said He would do, but after a great deal of time had passed, and God's promises had still not manifested, these believers were tempted to throw away (*apoballo*) their bold declaration of faith.

Not only were they tired of waiting, but they were also tired of voicing real bold faith (*parresia*). It was as if their lives were on pause and all forward movement had ceased. They had been sitting in the same place, waiting and waiting for God's promises to come to pass, but they hadn't seen the manifestation of anything yet.

Discouraged beyond words, they were tempted to grab hold of their real, bold, confident faith and hurl it so far away from them that they could no longer reach over and pick it up again. They were on the verge of discarding what they had been believing so that they could move on with their lives. It was at this point the writer of Hebrews said, "Cast not away therefore your confidence, which hath great recompence of reward" (Hebrews 10:35).

Your Faith Has 'Great Recompence of Reward'

The reason we are not to throw away our bold, forthright declaration of faith is because it "...hath great recompence of reward" (Hebrews 10:35). This phrase, "great recompence of reward" is a translation of the Greek word *misthapodosia*, which is a compound of the words *mistha* and *podosia*. The word *mistha* means *payment*, *salary*, or *reward*; and the word *podosia* comes from the word *podos*, which is the word for *feet*.

When we compound the words *mistha* and *podosia* to form *misthapodosia*, it depicts *payment* or *reward that has feet*. Inserting this meaning into Hebrews 10:35, we could translate the verse to say, "Hey, don't give up and let go of your faith declaration because the reward payment for staying in your place of faith is walking toward you right now! What you've been waiting for is on its feet and headed in your direction!"

Right now, you may be in a place just like these Hebrew believers. You may be discouraged, exhausted, and thinking about giving up on God's promise. Maybe you've been waiting and believing for healing, financial provision, or a breakthrough in your marriage, but nothing seems to be happening. God is saying to you, "Don't give up on the promise I've given you! Healing belongs to you! According to Isaiah 53:5, by Jesus' stripes, you are healed! Prosperity belongs to you! You were illuminated with Galatians 6:7, and you will reap what you've sown. And relational restoration belongs to you! I have blessed your marriage, and I'm able to restore it better than before!"

Friend, whatever God promised He will deliver. "God is not a man, so he does not lie. He is not human, so he does not change his mind. Has he ever spoken and failed to act? Has he ever promised and not carried it through?" (Numbers 23:19 *NLT*) Indeed, "...He is faithful that promised" (Hebrews 10:23).

The "great recompence of reward" — the Greek word *misthapodosia* — that you've been waiting for is it's on its feet and moving in your direction right now. But you need to stay where you're supposed to be so that when it shows up, you are there to receive it.

We Have 'Need of Patience'

Just after the writer of Hebrews informed his readers that the reward they were waiting for was on its way, he made a statement that few, if any, of us want to hear. He said:

> **For ye have need of patience, that, after ye have done the will of God, ye might receive the promise.**
> **— Hebrews 10:36**

More than likely, when the Jewish believers heard that they were in "need of patience," it probably wasn't received very well. Let's face it, no one gets excited about patience, because no one wants to go through the effort to develop it. Yet, we still *need* it.

This word "need" is the Greek word *chreian*, and it describes *a deficit, necessity, lack,* or *requirement.* Even though these Hebrew believers had waited a long time and demonstrated an ability to wait, they still had a deficit or lack of patience.

What's interesting is that the word "patience" here is the same word translated "endured" in Hebrews 10:32. It is the Greek word *hupomeno*, a compound word made up of the words *hupo*, which depicts *being under something*, and *meno*, which means *to stay* or *to abide*. When these two words are joined to form *hupomeno*, the resulting word depicts *a person who is under a very heavy load, but he has made a decision that despite the weight and pressure, he will not move.*

In a military sense, the word *hupomeno* was used to describe soldiers who were commanded to maintain the territory they had gained regardless of the opposition that came against them. In the same way, we need to be determined to maintain what God has promised us. Even if all hell comes against us, we must refuse to surrender. That's what this word "patience" means.

Having Patience Guarantees Victory

The Early Church called "patience" (*hupomeno*) the queen of all virtues because they knew if you have patience, it's not a question of *if* you're going to win — it's a question of *when*.

When the writer of Hebrews said, "For ye have need of patience," he was essentially saying, "You have need of *endurance* because there is a deficit of it in your life." Keep in mind endurance is the commitment to stay put regardless of how long it takes or how many obstacles come against you.

As you develop and operate in endurance (*hupomeno*), the enemy will eventually realize he is wasting his time on you. He's tried to break you and push you out of your place of faith, but you've been immovable. The moment he leaves you and goes to bother someone else is usually the time your answer comes. So don't move from your place of faith when you're on the brink of a breakthrough.

When you refuse to cast away your confidence, "a great recompense of reward" is on its way! That means your answer is already on its feet and moving in your direction, which is why it is so important that you stay where God has placed you and continue to hold fast to what He promised.

When You've Received the Promise, Your Wait Is Over

Looking again at Hebrews 10:36, we read, "For ye have need of patience, that, after ye have done the will of God, ye might receive the promise." Now, you may be asking, "How long am I supposed to stay in my place of faith? I've already been waiting for a very long time. How much longer does God expect me to wait and stay in this place of faith?"

The answer to that question is in Hebrews 10:36. It says, "...That, after ye have done the will of God, ye might receive the promise." You're not done until you've *received the promise*. The word "received" here is *komidzo*, which means *to be paid*. You don't leave your place of faith until you've been fully paid with God's promise.

- Has payday come for you regarding your *healing*? If not, stay put.

- Has payday come for you regarding the *salvation of your spouse, your child*, or *your friend*? If not, keep holding on to God's promise.

- Has payday come for you regarding *your dream becoming reality*? If not, stay in your place of faith.

You're not done until payday has come and you've received what God promised. That's how long you're supposed to wait.

The Promise Will Be Here Shortly

Next, the writer of Hebrews added, "For yet a little while, and he that shall come will come, and will not tarry" (Hebrews 10:37). The word "he" in this verse is the Greek word *ho*, which would better be translated as *the thing*. Hence, after a little while, *the thing* you've been waiting for shall come.

This brings us to the word "little"—the Greek word *mikron*, which is the term from which the English word *microscope* is derived. It means *small*, *little*, or *least*. In just *a little*, *microscopic* period of time, the thing you've been trusting God to bring to pass will come, and it will not *tarry*.

The word "tarry" here is the Greek word *chronidzo*, which means *to be late* or *to be delayed*. What God has promised is not going to be late or delayed. It's going to be on time. It's already on its feet and headed in your direction, and it will be here in a microscopic amount of time.

Friend, if you've been waiting and waiting for something, what's it going to hurt if you wait just a little bit longer? The thing you've been believing for is on its way!

Are There Consequences for Not Waiting?

The writer of Hebrews wrapped up Chapter 10 by saying, "Now the just shall live by faith: But if any man draw back, my soul shall have no pleasure in him. But we are not of them who draw back unto perdition; but of them that believe to the saving of the soul" (Hebrews 10:38-39). These verses speak of the consequences of drawing back from our place of faith and no longer believing that God's answer is on its way.

In the next lesson, we will dive into Hebrews 10:38-39. The writer of Hebrews used very vivid language to express how important it was that these new believers understand the weight of their decision to remain in faith.

STUDY QUESTIONS

> Study to shew thyself approved unto God, a workman that
> needeth not to be ashamed, rightly dividing the word of truth.
> — 2 Timothy 2:15

1. Can God's Word be trusted? *Absolutely!* To help increase your confidence in what God said in His Word, read these passages in a few different Bible translations and jot down the version the Holy Spirit illuminates in your heart:

   - **God does not lie.** (Numbers 23:19; Titus 1:2; Hebrews 6:18)

   - **God keeps His promises.** (1 Kings 8:56; Ezekiel 12:25; 2 Corinthians 1:20)

   - **God's Words are true and pure.** (2 Samuel 7:28; Psalm 12:6: 111:7)

   - **God's Word will never pass away.** (Matthew 5:18; 24:35; Luke 21:33)

2. What are the benefits of *trusting* in the Lord? What happens when you trust Him? Carefully consider these scriptures and allow the Holy Spirit to show you the value of trusting God.

   - Psalm 34:8 and 84:12

   - Psalm 32:10 and 125:1

   - Psalm 37:3-6

   - Proverbs 3:5-8 and 29:25

   - Isaiah 26:3-4

   - Jeremiah 17:7-8

PRACTICAL APPLICATION

> But be ye doers of the word, and not hearers only,
> deceiving your own selves.
> — James 1:22

1. The believers addressed in the book of Hebrews had initially been voicing their faith with bold confidence. But after a great deal of time had passed and God's promise still hadn't manifested, they were tempted to throw away their declaration of faith. Is there a bold declaration of faith that you've stopped voicing? If so, what is it? Take

a few moments to pray and ask the Holy Spirit to rekindle the fire of hope that God will bring His promises to pass in just a little while.

2. Although the Hebrew believers had been believing God's promises for a long time and had demonstrated an ability to wait, they still had a deficit or lack of patience. How about you? Would you say you are a *patient* or *impatient* person? If you see that you "have need of patience," don't feel condemned. Simply go to the Lord in prayer and say:

Father, I repent for my impatience as I wait for the manifestation of what You've promised. Please forgive me. Help me trust You to do what You said You would do. And help me learn to wait with a good attitude so that I can cultivate patience and build character. Thank You, Father, for loving me and being patient with me. In Jesus' name, amen!

LESSON 9

TOPIC

Is Your Faith Growing or Rotting?

SCRIPTURES

1. **Hebrews 10:35** — Cast not away therefore your confidence, which hath great recompence of reward.

2. **Mark 10:50** — And he, casting away his garment, rose, and came to Jesus.

3. **Hebrews 10:36-37** — For ye have need of patience, that, after ye have done the will of God, ye might receive the promise. For yet a little while, and he that shall come will come, and will not tarry.

4. **Hebrews 10:38-39** — Now the just shall live by faith: But if any man draw back, my soul shall have no pleasure in him. But we are not of them who draw back unto perdition; but of them that believe to the saving of the soul.

5. **Hebrews 11:1-2** — Now faith is the substance of things hoped for, the evidence of things not seen. For by it the elders obtained a good report.

GREEK WORDS

1. "cast not away" — ἀποβάλλω (*apoballo*): ἀπο (*apo*), which means away, and the word βάλλω (*ballo*), meaning to throw; as a compound, ἀποβάλλω (*apoballo*) is to throw off or to cast away

2. "confidence" — παρρησία (*parresia*): a bold, frank, forthright kind of speech; a declaration

3. "great recompence of reward" — μισθαποδοσία (*misthapodosia*): a compound of the words μισθα(*mistha*), meaning payment, salary, or reward; and ποδοσία (*podosia*) that comes from the word ποδοσ (*podos*), which is the word for feet

4. "need" — χρεία (*chreian*): a deficit, necessity, lack, requirement

5. "patience" — ὑπομένω (*hupomeno*): a compound word made up of the words ὑπο (*hupo*), which depicts being under something, and μένω (*meno*), which means to stay or to abide; the resulting compound word depicts a person who is under a very heavy load, but he has made a decision that despite the weight and pressure, he will not move; one man translated ὑπομένω (*hupomeno*) as hang-in-there power; another man translated it as staying power; ὑπομένω (*hupomeno*) also depicts soldiers who have been commanded maintain the territory they had gained, regardless of any resistance; the Early Church called ὑπομένω (*hupomeno*) the queen of all virtues

6. "receive" — κομίζω (*komidzo*): to be paid

7. "little" — μικρὸν (*mikron*): the word from which the English word microscope is derived; small, little, least

8. "faith" — πίστις (*pistis*): faith, belief, trust, confidence, fidelity; something forceful like a bullet shot out of a gun

9. "draw back" — ὑποστέλλω (*hupostello*): a compound word made up of ὑπο (*hupo*) and στέλλω (*stello*); στέλλω (*stello*) means to send, but when attached to ὑπο (*hupo*), it means to send back, to draw back, to withdraw, to retreat

10. "believe" — πίστις (*pistis*): faith, belief, trust, confidence, fidelity; something forceful like a bullet shot out of a gun

11. "perdition" — ἀπώλεια (*apoleia*): rot; depicts the result of leaving meat out to thaw and forgetting about it; destruction, ruin, loss

12. "now" — δέ (*de*): but, and, moreover, on the other hand

13. "substance" — ὑπόστασις (*hupostasis*): a compound word made up of ὑπό (*hupo*) and στασις (*stasis*); in this case, ὑπό (*hupo*) means by, and

στασις (*stasis*), which is a form of the word ἵστημι (*histemi*), means to stand; the compound word ὑπόστασις (*hupostasis*) means to stand by

14. "hoped for" — ἐλπίδος (*elpidos*): derived from the word ἐλπίς (*elpis*), which is the word for hope or expectation; a full expectation that what God has promised will come to pass

15. "elders" — πρεσβύτερος (*presbuteros*): refers to the spiritual leaders of the Old Testament

SYNOPSIS

Have you ever been around people whose lives just seem to *stink* — people whose attitudes, actions, and words all seem to emit a "foul smell" that you can't wait to get away from. What you may be getting a "whiff" of is a life marked by doubt, unbelief, and disobedience. As we will see in this lesson, the Bible makes it clear that when we are not operating in the place of faith where God has called us to live, a spiritual decay is set in motion that puts us in a rotten situation.

The emphasis of this lesson:

Real faith always has a forward motion. When we're moving in faith, we're growing and moving toward the promises of God. If we're in doubt and unbelief, we're moving in retreat, which left unchecked will produce a spiritual rottenness in our life. Real faith stands by the things hoped for and won't move.

The Hebrew Believers
Were About To Throw Away Their Faith

Returning to Hebrews 10:35, we read, "Cast not away therefore your confidence, which hath great recompence of reward." In this passage, we are given a promise — if we hold fast to our confidence, we will receive a great recompence of reward. Our part is to "cast not away our bold confession of faith.

The phrase "cast not away" is the Greek word *apoballo*, a compound of the words *apo* and *ballo*. The word *apo* means *away*, and the word *ballo* means *to throw*. When compounded, the new word *apoballo* means *to throw away*, *to discard*, or *to hurl far from you*.

We've seen that this word is also used in Mark 10:50 to describe a blind man named Bartimaeus who wanted to get up and go to Jesus, but he couldn't move because his garment was entangled around him. Motivated by Jesus' invitation to come to Him, Bartimaeus took his garment and *hurled it out of the way*. His bold actions declared, "I'm tired of this garment stopping me and keeping me in this place." Once it was discarded, he could finally move.

When we insert this meaning into the context of Hebrews 10:35, we see that these discouraged believers were on the verge of grabbing their faith in God's word and hurling it far from them — in the same way Bartimaeus grabbed his garment and hurled it away. They had been waiting and waiting for God's promise to come to pass, but because nothing had manifested, they were weary and tempted to toss it into the trash and move on with their lives.

Have you ever felt that way? Do you feel that way now? Are you so frustrated and worn out from waiting that you are ready to "cast away your confidence" in God's word to you? That's how these Jewish believers were feeling. In Hebrews 10:35, the Bible refers to their faith as "confidence," which is the Greek word *parresia*, describing *a bold, frank, forthright kind of speech*.

The use of this word *parresia* tells us clearly that faith always speaks. It has a voice, and when faith speaks, it's *bold*, *frank*, and *confident*. That is how these Hebrew believers had been speaking for quite some time — they were boldly and confidently confessing what God had said He was going to do in their lives. But because His promise hadn't manifested, they were thinking about throwing their faith away (*apoballo*) so they could just move on with their lives.

Our Faith Has 'Great Recompence of Reward'

The writer of Hebrews urged his readers not to throw away their bold confession of faith, because it carried a "...great recompence of reward" (Hebrews 10:35). In previous lessons, we learned that the phrase "great recompence of reward" is a translation of the Greek word *misthapodosia*, a compound of the words *mistha* and *podosia*. The word *mistha* always describes *payment*, *salary*, or *reward*; and the word *podosia* comes from the word *podos*, which is the word for *feet*.

When we put these two words together to form the word *misthapodosia*, it means *the reward, the payment, or the compensation that you've been waiting for is already on its feet, and it's moving in your direction.* Thus, the writer of Hebrews was telling his readers, "The answer is almost there! You're on the verge of receiving God's promise! Now is not the time to bail out."

Understand that when your mind and emotions come under satanic assault and you become weary, that is usually when you're just on the edge of your breakthrough. The answer you've been longing for in prayer is on its feet and moving in your direction. This is not the time to give up. It is the time to press into God's presence, pour out your heart, and ask Him for His grace to stay in your place of faith.

We Need 'Patience' To Receive God's Promises

How do we hold on when all hell seems to be coming against us? The writer of Hebrews wrote, "For ye have need of patience…" (Hebrews 10:36). The word "need" here is the Greek word *chreian*, and it describes *a deficit* or *a lack*. These Jewish believers had a deficit or lack of "patience." Again, this is the remarkable Greek word *hupomeno*, a compound of the words *hupo* and *meno*.

The word *hupo* depicts *being under something very heavy*, and *meno* means *I stay* or *I abide*. When these words are compounded, the new word depicts *a person who is under a very heavy load*, but he has made a decision that no matter how heavy the load gets or how much pressure comes on him, *he will not budge, flinch, or move from his place.*

This word *hupomeno* describes *hang-in-there power* or *staying power*. This word was also used in a military sense to describe soldiers who were commanded to maintain their territory and whatever ground that had been gained, regardless of how many assaults came against them. According to Hebrews 10:36, we need patience (*hupomeno*) if we want to receive the "great recompence of reward" that is promised to us.

Of course, the Hebrew believers who heard this probably didn't appreciate it because they had been waiting so long for God's promise to come to pass. The truth is none of us wants to talk about or take the time to develop patience, but we all desperately need it.

Actually, the word "patience" — the Greek word *hupomeno* — would better be translated *endurance*. It is the ability to stay put and hang in there until all resistance dissipates and disappears. It's at that moment that what you've been believing for shows up. Because of this, *hupomeno* (patience or endurance) was called the "queen of all virtues" by the Early Church.

Hold On!
Payday Is Coming Soon!

Looking once more at Hebrews 10:36, we read, "For ye have need of patience, that, after ye have done the will of God, ye might *receive the promise.*" It is interesting to note that the word "receive" is the Greek word *komidzo*, which is a word related to money or compensation just like the phrase "great recompence of reward" (*misthapodosia*).

In this case, the word *komidzo* — translated here as "receive" — means *to be paid*. So, when we look at Hebrew 10:35 and 36, we can know with certainty that payday is coming! In fact, the reward or compensation for us staying in our place of faith and trusting God is on its feet and moving in our direction. We just need endurance (*hupomeno*) to hang in there a little bit longer until we are paid.

Friend, when payday comes, you're going to be so glad you didn't bail out and cast away (*apoballo*) your bold confession of faith!

You may ask, "How long do I need to wait?" Good question! The answer is found in Hebrews 10:37, which says, "For yet a little while, and he that shall come will come, and will not tarry." The word "little" in Greek is *mikron*, which is where we get the English word *microscope*. It means *small*, *little*, or *least*. The use of this word *mikron* in Hebrews 10:37 lets us know that in a tiny, microscopic amount of time, the thing you've been believing for is going to show up, and it will not be late!

Staying in Faith
Means Moving Forward

The writer of Hebrews begins his wrap-up in chapter 10 with this declaration:

Now the just shall live by faith....

— Hebrews 10:38

The word "faith" here is the Greek word *pistis*, which denotes *faith, belief, trust, confidence*, or *fidelity*. It describes something forceful like a bullet shot out of a gun. Real faith always has a forward motion. When you're moving in faith, you're always moving forward. That is one way you can determine whether you're operating in faith. If you are moving forward toward your goal or toward what you're believing for, then you are in your place of faith.

Hebrews 10:38 goes on to say:

...But if any man draw back, my soul shall have no pleasure in him.

The words "draw back" in Greek translated from the Greek word *hupostello*, a compound word made up of *hupo* and *stello*. The word *stello* means *to send*, but when attached to *hupo*, it means *to send back, to draw back, to withdraw*, or *to retreat*. Therefore, a person who draws back is in retreat.

Keep in mind, faith is like a bullet shot out of a gun. If you're moving in faith, you're moving forward toward the promises of God. But if you're operating in doubt and unbelief, you're moving in reverse or retreat. Again, this is a way you can determine whether you're in faith. If you are in faith, you're on target and moving forward. If you are in retreat, then you're no longer in faith.

Withdrawing From Faith Produces Spiritual Rottenness

The Bible says in Hebrews 10:39, "But we are not of them who draw back unto perdition; but of them that believe to the saving of the soul." The words "draw back" are again the Greek word *hupostello*, which describes *retreat*. So the writer is saying, "We are *not* among those that are pulling back and retreating. We are among those that believe to the saving of the soul."

Interestingly, the word "believe" here is the Greek word *pistis* — the same word translated as "faith" in Hebrews 10:38. To be "of them that believe," means we have and are holding onto *faith, belief, trust*, and *confidence*, and that belief is like a bullet that has been forcefully shot out of a gun. Once it has been released, real faith never retreats. Remember, if you are in retreat, then you're no longer in faith.

Hebrews 10:39 says that those who are not in faith "...draw back unto perdition." The word "perdition" is the very intriguing Greek word *apoleia*, which describes *rot*. The best way to explain the meaning of this word *apoleia* is to imagine leaving meat outside to thaw and forgetting about it for several days. That meat would become rotten (*apoleia*). It would develop an appalling stench and likely be infested with maggots when you finally come back to it.

That is the word used in Hebrews 10:39 to describe a person who is no longer in a place of faith but instead, he "draws back" (*hupostello*) into "perdition" (*apoleia*). For some reason, that person has decided to throw away (*apoballo*) his confession of faith and withdraw from the promises of God he once believed. The consequence of such actions is a spiritual rottenness in that person's life.

Do You Know Someone Who Is No Longer in Faith?

Rick told the story of a person he met with over breakfast who was no longer in his place of faith. The man explained how there was a time in his life when he was really moving forward in faith. He was so confident as he declared God's Word boldly, and he was hopeful as he waited for the Lord to come through on His promises.

But something happened that brought the man to a place where he began to doubt the truth of God's Word and believe that what he was holding onto was nothing more than a fantasy. That doubt and unbelief grew so strong he decided to throw his faith away (*apoballo*).

"People who believe in faith are so deceived," were the shocking words that came from his mouth. They had a rotten "stench" that was sickening. This man, who at one time was so vibrant in his faith, now had a faith that was filled with maggots, so to speak.

Rick spoke of another man, someone he was once friends with, who had also abandoned his place of faith. At one time this person really had a precious relationship with God. But because of disappointments over the years, rather than hold fast his confidence, he chose to cast away (*apoballo*) his faith. The results of drawing back and retreating from trusting God's Word were stunning.

Rick said, "I was so shocked at what I heard coming out of his mouth that I almost started to cry. I thought, *How can this possibly be the same person I used to know?* This was a man who used to speak so tenderly about the Lord, his faith, and the work of Christ on the Cross. Now when he opened his mouth, only rot and filth were coming out."

That is what happens when a person who used to move in faith casts their faith away and begins moving in retreat. According to Hebrews 10:39, the condition of "perdition" sets in — the Greek word *apoleia*. What was once fresh and wholesome turns to rot and ruin, and in a sense, that person becomes spiritually disgusting.

Maybe you know someone like that — someone who once moved in faith, but because of various trials and troubles, he or she began moving in retreat. If you do, you need to pray for that person to have a turnaround. At the same time, you need to stop and look at your own life and ask yourself, "Am I still moving forward in faith, or am I in retreat? Am I moving toward what God promised, or am I backing away from it?"

If you are moving in retreat, away from what God promised, you are moving in the wrong direction, and it's time to make a course correction! It's time to repent and return to your place of faith "…so that times of refreshing may come from the presence of the Lord" (Acts 3:19 *NKJV*).

Understanding How Faith Behaves

The writer continued his teaching about faith in Chapter 11, declaring this often-quoted verse:

> **Now faith is the substance of things hoped for, the evidence of things not seen.**
>
> **— Hebrews 11:1**

What many people don't know about this verse is that the word "now" does not appear in the Greek text. Instead, we find the little Greek word *de*, which would be better translated as *but, and, moreover*, or *on the other hand*. When we insert the meaning of the word *de* into the verse, we could translate it:

> **Now, *on the other hand*, faith is the substance of things hoped for, the evidence of things not seen.**

Although many see Hebrews 11:1 as a definition of faith, it actually describes the *behavior* of faith. Interestingly, the word "substance" is a very poor translation of what the original text says. In Greek, the word "substance" is *hupostasis*, a compound of the words *hupo* and *stasis*. In this verse, the word *hupo* means *by*, and *stasis*, which is a form of the word *histemi*, means *to stand*. When compounded to form *hupostasis*, it means *to stand by something*. Hence, a better rendering would be:

Now, on the other hand, faith *stands by* things hoped for....

That is how faith behaves. Faith doesn't move. Faith doesn't budge. Faith never surrenders. It is like a bulldog that has wrapped its jowls around the bone of its dreams. Faith locks onto God's promise — His pledge and His Word — and never lets it go!

And just like a bulldog tenaciously clutches his bone in his mouth and will never let go, bulldog faith gets an iron-grip on what God said and will not let it loose. The devil can tug, prod, push, and pressure, but bulldog faith *stands by* things hoped for rather than moving into retreat.

This brings us to the words "hoped for," which are translated from the Greek word *elpidos*. It is derived from the word *elpis*, which is the term for *hope* or *expectation*. In this verse, it denotes *a full expectation that what God has promised will come to pass*. Rather than being a "hope so," it is a "know so," and the person standing by the thing "hoped for" is fully expecting and fully anticipating it to arrive at any moment. He has locked onto God's promise and is standing by what He said, refusing to budge from it.

The Old Testament 'Elders' Had Bulldog Faith

The writer of Hebrews went on to say, "For by it the elders obtained a good report" (Hebrews 11:2). By *what* did the elders obtain a good report? By this bulldog kind of faith — a faith that never budges, never flinches, and never lets go — the elders obtained a good report. The word "elders" here is the Greek word *presbuteros*, and it refers to *the spiritual leaders of the Old Testament*.

What we will see in our final lesson is that most of Hebrews 11 is about the Jewish patriarchs and history makers like Enoch, Noah, Abraham, and Moses. These are the individuals referred to as "elders" in verse 2, and all of them had to stand by the word God gave them. Life's circumstances and the devil tried to take it away, but they wrapped their jowls around what God had promised and refused to let go. They stood by what God had said, and as a result, they received the manifestation. And so can you!

STUDY QUESTIONS

> **Study to shew thyself approved unto God, a workman that**
> **needeth not to be ashamed, rightly dividing the word of truth.**
> **— 2 Timothy 2:15**

Being in faith produces spiritual growth, but drawing back and retreating from faith in the promises of God leads to spiritual decay. Take time to reflect on these passages where God talks about preserving, keeping, and protecting your life.

1. What do all these verses say about being preserved and kept?
   - Psalm 31:23-24; 32:7; 37:28; 97:10
   - Proverbs 2:8
   - 1 Thessalonians 5:23
   - 2 Timothy 4:18

2. What attribute is mentioned in each passage that preserves and keeps us from spiritual decay?
   - Psalm 25:21
   - Psalm 40:11
   - Psalm 41:1-3
   - Psalm 145:20
   - Proverbs 4:5-7

3. In addition to drawing back from a place of faith, there is something else the Bible warns about that can cause believers to enter a state of "perdition" (*apoleia*). Carefully read First Timothy 6:6-12 and identify this hazard and the strategy Paul gives for avoiding it.

PRACTICAL APPLICATION

> **But be ye doers of the word, and not hearers only,**
> **deceiving your own selves.**
> **— James 1:22**

1. In your own words, describe what it looks like to live *in faith* compared to what it looks like to live *in retreat*. What are the signs associated with each? In all honesty, what do the conditions of your

life reveal? Are you living and moving in faith or in retreat? Are you moving toward what God promised or backing away from it?

2. Do you know someone who once moved in faith but is now moving in retreat? If so, what is his or her life like? What caused that person to throw away his or her faith? Take time to pray for that person and ask the Holy Spirit for opportunities to encourage him or her to back on track.

3. Are you so frustrated and worn out from waiting that you're ready to "cast away your confidence" in God's word to you? What does the sobering thought of experiencing spiritual "rottenness" say to you about holding on to your faith and continuing to trust God to deliver on His promises?"

LESSON 10

TOPIC
Will Your Faith Change the Future?

SCRIPTURES

1. **Hebrews 10:23** — Let us hold fast the profession of our faith without wavering; (for he is faithful that promised).

2. **Hebrews 10:24** — And let us consider one another to provoke unto love and to good works.

3. **Hebrews 10:25** — Not forsaking the assembling of ourselves together, as the manner of some is; but exhorting one another....

4. **Hebrews 10:32,33** — But call to remembrance the former days, in which, after ye were illuminated, ye endured a great fight of afflictions; Partly, whilst ye were made a gazingstock....

5. **Hebrews 10:35** — Cast not away therefore your confidence, which hath great recompence of reward.

6. **Hebrews 10:36** — For ye have need of patience, that, after ye have done the will of God, ye might receive the promise.

7. **Hebrews 10:37** — For yet a little while, and he that shall come will come, and will not tarry.

8. **Hebrews 10:38** — Now the just shall live by faith: but if any man draw back, my soul shall have no pleasure in him.

9. **Hebrews 10:39** — But we are not of them who draw back unto perdition; but of them that believe to the saving of the soul.

10. **Hebrews 11:1** — Now faith is the substance of things hoped for, the evidence of things not seen.

11. **Hebrews 11:2** — For by it the elders obtained a good report.

12. **Hebrews 11:3** — Through faith we understand that the worlds were framed by the word of God, so that things which are seen were not made of things which do appear.

13. **Hebrews 11:6** — But without faith it is impossible to please him [God]….

GREEK WORDS

1. "another" — ἀλλήλων (*allelon*): describes reciprocal action; one another; each other

2. "exhorting" — παρακαλέω (*parakaleo*): a compound of the words παρα (*para*) and καλέω (*kaleo*); the word παρα (*para*) means alongside, as close as one can get, parallel; the word καλέω (*kaleo*) means to call; it describes one who calls out, beckons, or speaks; compounded, the new word παρακαλέω (*parakaleo*) describes one who comes alongside and speaks; this is the root word in παράκλητος (*parakletos*), which is translated Comforter in reference to the Holy Spirit; παρακαλέω (*parakaleo*) was used in a military sense to depict a commanding officer who comes alongside his troops before a battle and stirs them to action with encouraging words

3. "illuminated" — φωτίζω (*photidzo*): where we get the English word for photograph; a brilliant flash of light that leaves a permanent and lasting impression

4. "gazingstock" — θεατρίζω (*theatridzo*): derived from θέατρον (*theatron*), meaning a theater or a place for public show

5. "confidence" — παρρησία (*parresia*): a bold, frank, forthright kind of speech; a declaration

6. "patience" — ὑπομένω (*hupomeno*): a compound word made up of the words ὑπο (*hupo*), which depicts being under something, and μένω (*meno*), which means to stay or to abide; the resulting compound word depicts a person who is under a very heavy load, but he has made a

decision that despite the weight and pressure, he will not move; one man translated ὑπομένω (*hupomeno*) as hang-in-there power; another man translated it as staying power; ὑπομένω (*hupomeno*) also depicts soldiers who have been commanded to maintain the territory they have gained, regardless of any resistance; the Early Church called ὑπομένω (*hupomeno*) the queen of all virtues

7. "receive" — κομίζω (*komidzo*): to be paid

8. "little" — μικρὸν (*mikron*): the word from which the English word microscope is derived; small, little, least

9. "draw back" — ὑποστέλλω (*hupostello*): a compound word made up of ὑπο (*hupo*) and στέλλω (*stello*); στέλλω (*stello*) means to send, but when attached to ὑπο (*hupo*), it means to send back, to draw back, to withdraw, to retreat

10. "perdition" — ἀπώλεια (*apoleia*): rot; depicts the result of leaving meat out to thaw and forgetting about it; destruction, ruin, loss

11. "substance" — ὑπόστασις (*hupostasis*): a compound word made up of ὑπό (*hupo*) and στασις (*stasis*); in this case, ὑπό (*hupo*) means by, and στασις (*stasis*), which is a form of the word ἵστημι (*histemi*), means to stand; the compound word ὑπόστασις (*hupostasis*) means to stand by

12. "worlds" — αἰῶνας (*aionas*): specific periods of time within the history of mankind; for example: a year, a decade, a century, a millennium

13. "framed" — καταρτίζω (*katartidzo*): to be adjusted

14. "without" — χωρίς (*choris*): to be on the outside; derived from the Greek root word χωρα (*chora*), meaning space or region

SYNOPSIS

The Bible says, "…God has dealt to each one a measure of faith" (Romans 12:3 *NKJV*). Therefore, all of us have faith, but what we choose to do with the faith we've been given is what determines whether we are ordinary people or extraordinary people.

Hebrews 11 has often been called the Bible's "Hall of Faith." It contains snapshots of ordinary men and women who received a promise from God and then used their faith to leave an extraordinary legacy that forever changed the world.

In this final lesson, we will look back over the major points we learned from our study in Hebrews 10 and then examine how the bulldog faith of the heroes of old forever altered their lives and legacies.

The emphasis of this lesson:

Real faith tenaciously stands by the promises of God until they are fulfilled. The Old Testament heroes of faith all had a word from God, and they stood by that word until it came to pass. By staying in their place of faith, they changed the world — and so can you!

A REVIEW OF OUR PREVIOUS LESSONS

We must guard against *dream thieves*.

Hebrews 10:23 says, "Let us hold fast the profession of our faith without wavering; (for he is faithful that promised)." In Lesson 1, we learned that to see God's promises become a reality in our lives, we must really take hold of them. This means holding them down and putting all our spiritual "weight" on top of them so that the dream thieves cannot take them away.

Dream Thief #1: *Time.* Time has a voice. The enemy will use the passage of time to speak to you and say things like, "If it was going to happen, surely it would have happened by now. You need to stop all this dreaming and get back to the real world." Indeed, time will try to get you to give up on God's promise.

Dream Thief #2: *Friends.* No doubt, your friends are concerned about you. If they see that you've been waiting for a long time for your dream to come to pass and nothing has happened, they may try to coax you out of waiting so you can move on with your life. It is vital for you to hold onto the dream and the word God gave you or your friends might talk you out of it.

Dream Thief #3: *Family.* Few people are closer to you and love you more than family. They really care about you, and out of their concern, they may say things like, "Are you sure God spoke to you? You have misunderstood Him in the past, so maybe you have misunderstood what He said in this situation. Maybe you shouldn't get your hopes up and just go on with your life." If you hear these kinds of things from you family, prayerfully go back over what God said, and hold fast to it.

Dream Thief #4: *The devil.* The voice of the devil himself will mock you and denigrate you for what you've been believing, telling you things like, "Nothing's happening, and nothing is going to happen. All you are is a self-exalted dreamer trying to elevate yourself above others. Give it up and get back to the real world!" Friend, don't believe the devil's lies. Hold fast to what God spoke to you and stay in agreement with Him.

Dream Thief #5: *Neutrality.* When you grow so tired of waiting for God to do what He said He would do, eventually, you come to a place where you say something like, "I couldn't care less if this *ever* happens." That's the voice of neutrality. If you're "slipping into neutral" concerning your God-given dream, it's time for you to wrap your arms around what He has said, and ask the Holy Spirit to fan into flames the fire you once had for the calling on your life.

Dream Thief #6: *Isolation.* When you live life alone and isolated, you become more vulnerable to *all* of the dream thieves. This is not God's will for your life. Instead, you were made to live in reciprocal relationships with other believers. Hebrews 10:24 says, "And let us consider one another to provoke unto love and to good works."

We need each other.

In Lesson 3, we learned why we need each other and discovered the meaning of Hebrews 10:24. We saw that the words "one another" are translated from the Greek word *allelon*, which describes *reciprocal action*. As a believer, you are part of the Body of Christ and called to be connected to a local church, part of a home group, or in relationship with other believers. They are to encourage you, and you are to encourage them.

In fact, this verse says we're to "…provoke [each other] unto love and to good works" (Hebrews 10:24). This provoking is not meant to get people into a confrontation. Instead, we're to come right alongside each other, get in a parallel position, and poke and prod one another to stay in our place of faith. This is especially true regarding those who are being tempted to give up. We are to say things like, "You've invested far too much time in this to walk away now. Besides, you're right on the brink of receiving your breakthrough. Don't give up! Hold fast to God's promises and stay in faith!"

We must exhort one another.

Next, Hebrews 10:25 teaches that we are to *exhort* one another: "Not forsaking the assembling of ourselves together, as the manner of some is; but exhorting one another...." We saw in Lessons 4 and 5 that the word "exhorting" is from the marvelous Greek word *parakaleo*, a compound of the words *para* and *kaleo*. The word *para* means *alongside* or *as close as one can get*, and it points to being *parallel* in relationship with other believers. The second word *kaleo* means *to call*, and it describes *one who calls out, beckons*, or *speaks*.

When we compound these words, the new word *parakaleo* — translated here as "exhorting" — describes *one who comes alongside another and speaks*. God has called you to come alongside fellow believers (*para*) and call out to them (*kaleo*), encouraging them to stay in their place of faith.

Furthermore, the word "exhorting" — *parakaleo* — was also a military term used to describe a captain or a general who would come alongside his troops and speak to them honestly about the battle they were about to enter and ready them for the fight.

In the same way, we as believers have the privilege of coming alongside others to stir them up in their faith, fight the good fight, and encourage them to hold fast to God's promises. Like the Holy Spirit exhorts us, we are to exhort others, with words like, "You can do it! You have everything you need to win. You're more than a conqueror in Christ, and thank God, He always leads you into victory!"

We must remember what God has said.

Hebrews 10:32 says, "But call to remembrance the former days, in which, after ye were illuminated, ye endured a great fight of afflictions." In Lessons 5 and 6, we took a close look at what it means to be "illuminated." In Greek, this is the word *photidzo*, which is from where we get the English words *photo* and *photograph*. It describes *a brilliant flash of light that leaves a permanent and lasting impression*. In this verse, the writer of Hebrews is telling us to dig up and dust off those precious memories in which God first spoke to us and gave us revelation of His truth. He wants us to set those "*photidzo*" moments on a pedestal and never forget how they changed our life.

We must prepare for a great fight.

Hebrews 10:32 also reveals that during those times of great illumination, we also "…endured a great fight of afflictions." Here we see that a great fight of affliction usually follows illumination. When we receive a word from God, it throws us into a fight with the enemy, and the "afflictions" he sends are attacks against our mind and emotions.

Realize that the devil is terrified of illuminated people because he knows that when you're illuminated, you have the power to change history. Rather than let you just march forward in your illumination with no resistance, he'll come against you with a great fight of affliction to try to stop you dead in your tracks.

We will be made into a public spectacle.

Next, we reviewed Hebrews 10:33, which says, "Partly, whilst ye were made a gazingstock…." One of the major ways the enemy attacks your mind and emotions is by making you a "gazingstock" to those around you. We learned in Lessons 6 and 7 that the word "gazingstock" is the Greek word *theatridzo*, and that it is derived from the word *theatron*, the term for *a theater* or *a place for public show*.

Strangely, before you receive a word from God, things are quiet, and no one notices you. But the moment you say that God spoke to you and made you a promise, you suddenly become a spectacle that everyone begins to watch. Scripture says you become like a theater (*theatridzo*) — a "gazingstock." It is as if people begin to buy tickets to the show to see if God really did speak to you or if you're just imagining things. Not only that, they watch to see if you have the tenacity and the endurance to make it all the way to the end.

So since people are filling the theater to watch your life, make sure you give them the best performance they've ever seen! Show them how faith works. Give them a demonstration of endurance (*hupomeno*). Show them how to stick it out, stay put, never give up, and outlast the enemy. Do it so well that by the time you get to the final act and you're standing in victory, they're going to want to get out of the seats and get on the stage themselves and do something for God!

We must not throw away our faith.

In Lessons 7 and 8, we looked closely at Hebrews 10:35, which says, "Cast not away therefore your confidence, which hath great recompence of reward." We learned that the Jewish believers had grown weary from waiting on God to fulfill His promises. In fact, they were so exhausted and discouraged that they were tempted to throw away (*apoballo*) their bold declaration of faith. Knowing this, the writer of Hebrews urged them, "Cast not away therefore your confidence...."

In Greek, the word "confidence" is the word *parresia*, which describes *a very bold, frank, forthright kind of speech*. That's how real faith speaks. Faith is never silent, and when you're really moving in faith, your mouth is declaring God's Word. That is what these Hebrew believers were about to "cast away," but the writer urged them not to because their bold faith — just like your faith — had "...great recompence of reward" (Hebrews 10:35). In Greek, this literally means the answer is on its feet and moving in your direction!

We have need of patience.

In Lessons 8 and 9, we learned of our need for patience. Hebrews 10:36 says, "For ye have need of patience, that, after ye have done the will of God, ye might receive the promise." We saw that the word "patience" here is the Greek word *hupomeno*, which is supernatural *endurance* or *hang-in-there power*. It is the picture of a person who is under a very heavy load, but he has made a decision that despite the weight and pressure, he will not move.

As we cooperate with the Holy Spirit and choose to stay in our place of faith and declare God's Word in faith, we will "receive the promise." The word "receive" here is *komidzo*, which means *to be paid*. We're not done until we've *received the promise*. We are to stay in our place of faith until we've been fully paid and are experiencing what God said.

We are on the edge of a breakthrough.

Many Christians often ask, "How long am I supposed to stay in my place of faith? I've already been waiting for a very long time." The answer is found in Hebrews 10:37: "For yet *a little while*, and he that shall come will come, and will not tarry." The word "he" here is the Greek word *ho*, which would better be translated as *the thing*. Hence, *the thing* you've been waiting for shall come after *a little while*.

In Greek, the word "little" is *mikron*, which describes *something small, little, or least*. It is the term from which the English word *microscope* is derived. Its use in Hebrews 10:37 indicates that in just a *little, microscopic* period of time, the thing you've been trusting God for will come, and it will not be late. Usually, the desire to give up and the enemy's attacks are strongest right when you're on the edge of receiving your breakthrough. So don't quit now. The answer is on the way. Payday is coming!

We must live by faith.

To receive all that God has for us, we must abide in a place of faith, which is why the writer of Hebrews declared, "Now the just shall live by faith…" (Hebrews 10:38). In Lesson 9, we saw that the word "faith" in this verse is the Greek word *pistis*, which describes *faith*, *belief*, *trust*, or *confidence*. It carries the idea of something forceful like a bullet shot out of a gun.

Real faith always has a forward motion. When you're moving in faith, you're always moving forward. That is one way you can determine whether you're operating in faith. If you're moving forward toward your goal or the promise God gave you, then you are in your place of faith.

Hebrews 10:38 goes on to say, "…But if any man draw back, my soul shall have no pleasure in him." The words "draw back" in Greek are *hupostello*, a compound of the words *hupo* and *stello*. The word *stello* means *to send*, but when attached to *hupo*, it means *to send back*, *to draw back*, *to withdraw*, or *to retreat*. Therefore, anyone not moving forward in faith is moving backward in retreat, which is the wrong direction to go and not pleasing to God.

We must not draw back.

Hebrews 10:39 says, "But we are not of them who draw back unto perdition; but of them that believe to the saving of the soul." The Bible is clear: Those who are *not* in faith "…draw back unto perdition…." We learned in our last lesson that the word "perdition" is the Greek word *apoleia*, which describes *rottenness* or *something foul and in a state of decay*. The use of this word here lets us know that when a person rejects his faith and "draws back" (*hupostello*) into "perdition" (*apoleia*), it creates a rotten, stinking spiritual condition in his life.

We must have 'bulldog' faith.

The writer of Hebrews continued teaching about faith in chapter 11, contrasting the difference between those who are NOT in faith with those who are IN faith. Hebrews 11:1says: "Now faith is the substance of things hoped for, the evidence of things not seen."

As we mentioned in Lesson 9, the word "now" does not appear in the Greek text. Instead, we see the little Greek word *de*, which would be better translated as *but* or *on the other hand*. Thus, a more accurate translation of Hebrews 11:1 would be, "*On the other hand*, faith is the substance of things hoped for, the evidence of things not seen."

Next, notice the word "substance," which in Greek is the word *hupostasis*. It is a compound of the words *hupo* and *stasis*, and in this particular passage, the word *hupo* means *by* and *stasis* means *to stand*. When we compound the words to form *hupostasis*, it means *to stand by something*. Hence, a better rendering of Hebrews 11:1 would be: "On the other hand, faith *stands by* things hoped for...."

That is how faith behaves. It is the picture of a person who says, "I know this is mine, and I'm not going to relinquish it. I'm going to stand by this, embrace it, and hold it tight. I don't care how hard others try to pull it away from me; I'm going to stand by this promise and never let it go until I see it fulfilled in my life."

Hebrews 11:1 describes the *behavior* of faith, not the definition of faith. Real faith doesn't move, doesn't budge, and never surrenders. It is like a bulldog that has wrapped its jaws around the bone of its dreams. That bulldog clenches down tight, and no matter how hard anyone pulls on that bone, that bulldog will never let it go.

In the same way, *bulldog* faith locks onto God's promises and never lets it go! The devil can push, prod, and pressure, but bulldog faith *stands by things hoped* for.

Many Heroes of the Faith Are Celebrated in Hebrews 11

In Hebrews 11:2, the writer went on to say, "For by it the elders obtained a good report." The "it" referred to here is the bulldog kind of faith we've been talking about. By tenacious, bulldog faith — a faith that is unbendable, unbreakable, and never gives up — the elders obtained a good report. The word "elders" here refers to *the spiritual leaders of the Old Testament*.

As we read Hebrews 11, we discover a "who's who" list of the great heroes of the faith, including Enoch, Noah, Abraham, Isaac, Jacob, Joseph, and Moses. All these people received a word from God and had to deal with great adversities that tried to take that word away. But like a bulldog on a bone, they wrapped their jowls around God's promise and said, "I'm going to stand by God's word, regardless of who comes against me or what happens in life to try and take it from me. I know God spoke to me, and I'm not going to let go of what He said!"

Their "bulldog" faith changed human history!

When we come to Hebrews 11:3, we read:

> **Through faith we understand that the worlds were framed by the word of God, so that things which are seen were not made of things which do appear.**

At first glance, this verse may seem a bit confusing or out of place. On the surface, it sounds like it's talking about creation, but a closer look at the original Greek text tells us otherwise.

Remember, much of Hebrews 10 is talking about faith, and the first two verses of Hebrews 11 talk about how faith behaves and how the elders, or Old Testament heroes, obtained a good report because of their faith. To think that the writer of Hebrews suddenly switched subjects in verse 3 and went all the way back to creation is incorrect. What we have in the *King James Version* of Hebrews 11:3 is a poor translation of a few key words.

Take, for example, the word "worlds." When the Bible says, "Through faith we understand that the *worlds* were framed," the word "worlds' is not the word *kosmos*, which refers to *the universe*, *the planet*, and *creation*. Instead, it is the Greek word *aionas*, which describes *specific periods of time within the history of mankind*.

For example, the word *aionas* might refer to *a year*, *a decade*, *a century*, or *a millennium*. It could even be *a generation*. Therefore, a more accurate translation of Hebrews 11:3 would be:

> **Through the unbendable, unbreakable, never-give-up kind of faith, we understand that *different time periods — different years, decades, centuries, millennia, and generations* — were framed by the word of God....**

Next, notice the word "framed." It is the Greek word *katartidzo*, and it means *to be adjusted*. When we take this meaning, along with the meaning of the word "worlds" (*aionas*), and we insert it into Hebrews 11:3, a more correct translation would be:

Through the unbendable, unbreakable, never-give-up kind of faith, we understand that different time periods — different years, decades, centuries, millennia, and generations — were *adjusted and altered* by the word of God....

How were these different time periods in history adjusted? By those elders — those Old Testament heroes — who received a word from God and stood by that word in faith until it became a reality. That is what the Greek actually states.

The rest of the verse goes on to say, "...So that things which are seen were not made of things which do appear." This means that by the time these Old Testament heroes came to the end of their life, they left the world completely different than the way they found it. Because they refused to budge or let go of God's promise to them in their time, in their generation, or in their day, they completely altered the course of history. That is the extraordinary power of you holding onto one promise from God.

We are given the amazing example of...

- *Enoch* in Hebrews 11:5.
- *Noah* in Hebrews 11:7.
- *Abraham* in Hebrews 11:8-10; 17-19.
- *Sarah* in Hebrews 11:11.
- *Isaac* in Hebrews 11:20.
- *Jacob* in Hebrews 11:21.
- *Joseph* in Hebrews 11:22.
- *Moses* in Hebrews 11:23-29.

All these individuals got a word from God and said, "I'm not letting go of this word! I'm going to stand by it, regardless of my age, my resources, or the hindrances that come against me. Without a doubt, I know that God spoke to me, and I'm not going to let go of what He said!"

What Does It Mean To Be 'Without Faith'?

This brings us to one of the most quoted verses of Scripture among Christians, which is Hebrews 11:6, where the writer of Hebrews declares:

But without faith it is impossible to please him [God]....

Many people read this passage and think it is talking about *having* or *not having* faith, but that is not what it means. A careful look at the original text reveals that the word "without" is the Greek word *choris*, which means *to be on the outside*. It is derived from the Greek root word *chora*, meaning *space* or *region*.

To understand the word *choris*, imagine you are standing outside in front of your house. You can see the roof, the windows, the garden, and the lawn, but what you can't see is anything inside the house. For you to enjoy and appreciate what's inside, you have to go *inside*. You can't be outside (without) and inside (within) the house at the same time.

In the same way, you can't be outside and inside your place of faith at the same time. You must choose one or the other. The word *choris* — translated here as "without" — means *to be on the outside*. Thus, a better translation of the first part of Hebrews 11:6 would be:

> **When you are *on the outside of faith*, it is impossible to please him** [God]....

The use of the word *choris* here tells us plainly that faith is *a place*. It is the place where you are abiding within the promise or pledge God gave you. That is what it means *to stay in your place of faith*.

The enemy will do all he can — using all the dream thieves at his disposal — to try and move you out of your place of faith. He knows that if he can get you to "cast away" (*apoballo*) your "confidence" (*parresia*) and "draw back" (*hupostello*) from what God said, you will be on the outside of faith (*choris*), and you can't please God.

Friend, it is essential that you stay in your place of faith. As long as you're in faith — holding onto and believing the promise or word God gave you — eventually the *dream thieves* will go away, and you will find yourself invaded by the manifestation of what you've been waiting for. May the Spirit of God give you the grace you need as you seek Him daily so that you can stay in your place of faith and experience the "great recompense of reward" He has for you!

STUDY QUESTIONS

**Study to shew thyself approved unto God, a workman that
needeth not to be ashamed, rightly dividing the word of truth.
— 2 Timothy 2:15**

1. As you come to the end of this study, what are two of your greatest
   takeaways regarding how to stay in a place of faith? What has the
   Holy Spirit been showing you that you really want to remember and
   share with others?

2. Of all the legendary Old Testament heroes mentioned in Hebrews 11,
   who do you most admire? What is it about that person's life that encourages you, inspires you, and challenges you to come up higher in your
   walk of faith with Jesus?

PRACTICAL APPLICATION

**But be ye doers of the word, and not hearers only,
deceiving your own selves.
— James 1:22**

1. Imagine your best friend is a new Christian and he or she is hungry
   to understand what faith is and how to move in it. Using what you
   have learned in these lessons, how might you describe how real faith
   behaves?

2. Hebrews 11:6 says, "But without faith it is impossible to please him
   [God]...." Prior to this lesson, what did you understand this verse to
   mean? How does this teaching — that faith is a *location* we can live
   "in" or "out" of — change the way you understand this passage?

3. Do you know God's primary purpose for your life? If so, what do you
   believe it to be, and are you living "in" or "out" of your place of faith? If
   you don't know what God has called you to do with your life, consider
   using your talents to help someone else accomplish what he or she is
   doing for God until He makes your calling clear? You are His "sheep,"
   and you can hear His voice (*see* John 10:27). As you seek Him and
   obey what He tells you, He will instruct you and teach you in the way
   you should go (*see* Psalm 32:8).

A Prayer To Receive Salvation

If you've never received Jesus as your Savior and Lord, now is the time for you to experience the new life Jesus wants to give you! To receive God's gift of salvation that can be obtained through Jesus alone, pray this prayer from your heart:

Jesus, I repent of my sin and receive You as my Savior and Lord. Wash away my sin with Your precious blood and make me completely new. I thank You that my sin is removed, and Satan no longer has any right to lay claim on me. Through Your empowering grace, I faithfully promise that I will serve You as my Lord for the rest of my life.

If you just prayed this prayer of salvation, you are born again! You are a brand-new creation in Christ! Would you please let us know of your decision by going to **renner.org/salvation**? We would love to connect with you and pray for you as you begin your new life in Christ.

Scriptures for further study: John 3:16; John 14:6; Acts 4:12; Ephesians 1:7; Hebrews 10:19,20; 1 Peter 1:18,19; Romans 10:9,10; Colossians 1:13; 2 Corinthians 5:17; Romans 6:4; 1 Peter 1:3

A Note From Rick Renner

I am on a personal quest to see a "revival of the Bible" so people can establish their lives on a firm foundation that will stand strong and endure the test as end-time storm winds begin to intensify.

In order to experience a revival of the Bible in your personal life, it is important to take time each day to read, receive, and apply its truths to your life. James tells us that if we will continue in the perfect law of liberty — refusing to be forgetful hearers, but determined to be doers — we will be blessed in our ways. As you watch or listen to the programs in this series and work through this corresponding study guide, I trust you will search the Scriptures and allow the Holy Spirit to help you hear something new from God's Word that applies specifically to your life. I encourage you to be a doer of the Word He reveals to you. Whatever the cost, I assure you — it will be worth it.

> Thy words were found, and I did eat them;
> and thy word was unto me the joy and rejoicing of mine heart:
> for I am called by thy name, O Lord God of hosts.
> — Jeremiah 15:16

Your brother and friend in Jesus Christ,

Rick Renner

Unless otherwise indicated, all scripture quotations are taken from the *King James Version* of the Bible.

Scripture quotations marked (*AMPC*) are taken from the *Amplified® Bible, Classic Edition*. Copyright © 1954, 1958, 1962, 1964, 1965, 1987 by The Lockman Foundation. Used by permission. **www.Lockman.org**

Scripture quotations marked (*NIV*) are taken from the *Holy Bible, New International Version®*, *NIV®* Copyright ©1973, 1978, 1984, 2011 by Biblica, Inc.® Used by permission. All rights reserved worldwide.

Scripture quotations marked (*NLT*) are taken from the Holy Bible, *New Living Translation*, copyright © 1996, 2004, 2015 by Tyndale House Foundation. Used by permission of Tyndale House Publishers, Inc., Carol Stream, Illinois 60188. All rights reserved.

How To Stay in a Place of Faith

Copyright © 2025 by Rick Renner
1814 W. Tacoma St.
Broken Arrow, OK 74012-1406

Published by Rick Renner Ministries
www.renner.org

ISBN 13: 978-1-6675-1250-1

eBook ISBN 13: 978-1-6675-1251-8

All rights reserved. No portion of this book may be reproduced or transmitted in any form or by any means — electronic, mechanical, photocopy, recording, scanning, or other — except for brief quotations in critical reviews or articles, without the prior written permission of the Publisher.

Notes

CLAIM YOUR FREE RESOURCE!

As a way of introducing you further to the teaching ministry of Rick Renner, we would like to send you FREE of charge his teaching, "How To Receive a Miraculous Touch From God" on CD or as an MP3 download.

How To Receive
a Miraculous Touch From God
Rick Renner

CD56

R RENNER

In His earthly ministry, Jesus commonly healed *all* who were sick of *all* their diseases. In this profound message, learn about the manifold dimensions of Christ's wisdom, goodness, power, and love toward all humanity who came to Him in faith with their needs.

☑ **YES, I want to receive Rick Renner's monthly teaching letter!**

Simply scan the QR code to claim this resource or go to: **renner.org/claim-your-free-offer**

Connect

WITH US!

R renner.org

f facebook.com/rickrenner • facebook.com/rennerdenise

▶ youtube.com/rennerministries • youtube.com/deniserenner

◉ instagram.com/rickrrenner • instagram.com/rennerministries_
instagram.com/rennerdenise

www.ingramcontent.com/pod-product-compliance
Lightning Source LLC
LaVergne TN
LVHW021403080426
835508LV00020B/2433